TOP
Self
Publishing
Firms

Top
Self
Publishing
Firms

How Writers Get Published,
Sell More Books, and
Rise to the Top
and
Make Money Working from Home
with the Best
Print On Demand
Self-Publishing Companies

by
Stacie Vander Pol

Printed in the United States of America

Published by
Pacific Publishing Studio

ISBN - 9781440407543

For bulk or wholesale orders, please send request to
the email address found at www.PacPS.com

Contact the author for reproduction requests, comments,
or corrections at www.PacPS.com

Contents

Book Pricing
Author Purchase Discounts
Author Rights and Contract
Additional Services

Title Your Book to Increase Sales
The Book Cover
Search Suggestions
Book Detail Page
Book Reviews
Author Profile
Amazon Blog
Listmania and Guides
Look Inside the Book

Blogging and Social Networking
Press Releases
Review Copies
A Website for Your Book
Google Adwords
Newswire Services
Writing a Press Release or Blog Entry

Bonus Chapter

Introduction

The first year this book came out became a historical year for publishing. The industry finally reached a long anticipated tipping point. In 2008, for the first time in history, the number of self-published titles brought to market exceeded the number of new traditionally published titles. Since then, the trend has grown stronger each year, with self-publishing edging out traditional houses at an increasingly greater margin. Though traditional publishers remain quite relevant, the trend *toward* self-publishing can no longer be ignored. What this means for traditional publishing houses is difficult to predict, but for the rest of us it means that the opportunity to thrive without a traditional publisher is increasingly abundant.

Even better, this changing of the guard so to speak has further increased the demand for high quality self-publishing options. Perhaps that's why the biggest names in publishing are making large investments in the self-publishers that do it well. Barnes & Noble, Random House, and Amazon.com all own significant stakes in self-publishing firms and this trend is growing.

The companies listed in this book have made it possible for *anyone* to publish retail quality books and sell them through retailers like Barnes & Noble and Amazon.com. Thousands of top selling titles, produced by the firms in this book, prove that self-published authors do succeed. You no longer need a big publisher, an agent, a publicist, and a marketing department to achieve success. You can choose your own publisher, be your own publicist and agent (*keeping their fees for yourself*), and let Amazon.com be your no-cost marketing department.

Publishing a book can make you an overnight authority in your field and give you expert status in your subject. Even if you don't make writing a full-time career, writing a book will increase your credibility in an advancing career or pave the road for a new one. It will also bring incredible gratification and satisfaction not found in other endeavors.

This is your ultimate resource to publishers that sell more books, offer the best distribution channels, and provide the greatest overall value for authors. You will also find information on the most cost effective and viable options based on your needs, goals, and budget.

A well crafted, self-published book can sell just as well as other books on the market and in many cases better, faster, and with more of the profit going to the one who deserves it... you! This book will help you succeed with your publishing goals and help you find a rewarding partnership with one of the top firms.

1
Success and Self-Publishing

Writing. I don't go through a single week without meeting someone, upon hearing what I do, tell me, "I've always thought about writing a book." Fortunately for those of us who make a living in publishing and writing, 99% of people will never get around to writing an entire book. For the few disciplined and determined enough to complete a manuscript, self-publishing is not only one of the best options, it's often the only *viable* option for an un-established writer to become a published author. Though the words *success* and *self-publishing* are not often associated with one another, many self-published authors have found the support they need to succeed by partnering with a self-publishing company.

In short, self-publishing firms are companies that help writers publish their books. They generally accept any and all manuscripts and will print and prepare a retail quality book that is indistinguishable from other books on the market. Not only do these firms produce a quality product, they provide an official ISBN number and place your book into the major distribution channels for bookstores, libraries, and online retailers.

These days, many firms can offer quality printing and binding as well as distribution, but only a select few are producing consistent sales results, year after year. This book profiles the top performing professional-level self-publishing firms, based largely on their sales results. Other factors in self-publishing are important, but *without sales none of them matter.* Book sales will determine how much money you make, how seriously you are taken as a writer, and how much recognition your book receives. All of the firms discussed are here because they have a track-record of success.

One thing this book does not do is spend time convincing you to choose self-publishing over traditional publishing. It assumes you have researched your options and have your reasons for using a self-publisher. Perhaps you are familiar with the highly unfavorable odds of being traditionally published, you're publishing time sensitive material, or you believe you can make more money through self-publishing. For me, it's all of the above. After successfully self-publishing several books and making a career out of writing and self-publishing, I can't see a good reason why an unknown author would bother with traditional publishing. But again, I'm not here to persuade you, just to provide the information you need to be successful.

Here you will find publishers with a proven history of success and impressive book sales. You will learn which firms are best for getting your book into stores like Barnes & Noble and which firms rock the charts on Amazon.com. You will also be able to compare royalty payments between each company based on real dollar amounts paid per book, not just the confusing (and often misleading) advertised percentages. You might be surprised to learn that many of the most successful publishers are also the most affordable.

Success Awaits You (but it's not guaranteed)

Everything you need to know about choosing a self-publisher and succeeding with your book will be covered in the chapters to follow. Because choosing a company is only half the battle, I've included a chapter on the genres that work best for self-published titles as well as a chapter on leveraging Amazon.com sales. This book will serve as a solid resource for both choosing a firm that most suits your needs and positioning yourself for success in the market.

Regardless of everything you'll learn here, nothing will substitute for a well written, engaging book. A self-publishing firm can level the playing field for access to sales, but it cannot negate the effects of the free market. Just because you *can* publish a book, doesn't necessarily mean that people will read it. The non-discriminate approach from self-publishing firms allows good writers the access they need to become successful authors. It also means thousands of worthless books are published each year by writers who aren't serious about success.

The ugly truth about self-publishing is that the majority of self-published books are so poorly written they aren't worth reading. The results are poor sales for poor books. Don't let your book fall into the large pile of underperforming self-published titles. If you want to rise to the top or even to the middle, you absolutely *must* write an excellent book. Invest in writing classes at your local community college, thoroughly research the demand for your subject before you write the book, and commit to numerous re-writes and edits before submitting your book for publication. A few books on writing and style that I strongly recommend are the lovely pocket-sized *Elements of Style,* the heftier but thorough *Chicago Manual of Style*, and a book I've recently taken a shine to, *Keys to Great Writing* by Stephen Wilbers.

Great Expectations

Once you have written a manuscript and selected a firm, you'll be ready to publish. You will submit your writing to your self-publisher electronically. Your word document (or other word processing document) will either be uploaded to your publisher's website or sent as an attachment through email. Your publisher will then convert your manuscript and format it for printing. Once the pages are set up, they will be printed and bound.

Either you or your publisher can design the book cover. Some firms offer a choice of templates to get you started. Others offer custom book cover design. In either case, your cover will be full color, unless you request otherwise. The ink colors, paper quality, cover stock, and bookbinding will be of professional quality, indistinguishable from other books.

Most readers will have no idea your book is self-published. It will look and feel just like other books, have a bar code printed on the back, and will be available through the regular distribution channels required for selling in stores. Your publisher will register your book with online retailers like Amazon.com and list it with major wholesalers like Ingram and Baker & Taylor.

You will not be responsible for storing books or fulfilling orders (unless you want to be). Print-on-demand technology (used by self-publishers) has made it possible to produce books one at a time, as they are ordered. You won't have to spend one penny, let alone thousands of dollars, on print runs. You won't have to guess how many books will sell. You just have to write your book, publish it, and collect your royalties. No inventory. No stacks of books in the garage. No wasted money. You can focus your efforts on writing and promoting your next book while your publisher handles printing and shipping, without any oversight from you.

Measuring Success

How does one measure success in publishing? It is more difficult than it should be. If publishers released their sales numbers to the public, measuring the success of a book or a firm would be easy. Unfortunately, neither the traditional nor the self-publishers disclose anything resembling detailed sales information. Accurate figures are a closely guarded secret in the industry, making it difficult to draw conclusions about sales success.

Amazon.com gives a sales rank to every book on their site. Most writers and many customers are familiar with the Amazon ranking; it can be found on every book detail page on the site. If you're unfamiliar with the Amazon ranking, I encourage you to go to Amazon.com and pull up your favorite book. Scroll down the book's main sales page until you come to a section called Product Details. Here you will find the page count, ISBN number, dimensions, as well as the Amazon.com Sales Rank. Though many authors obsess about their hourly Amazon ranking, the ranking tells nothing about the number of books sold, only how well one book is selling against another at that moment in time.

Amazon ranks over five million titles, though experts will tell you any book ranked at greater than one million isn't actually selling. (Perhaps this is why Nielsen BookScan tracks 1.2 million titles each year.) For the purposes of this book, I will dismiss the bottom four million and focus on the top one million titles on Amazon.

The Amazon sales rank places books in *order* of sales performance. For instance, the self-published book, *Practical Chess Exercises* currently ranks 2717. In other words, 2716 books are outselling *Practical Chess* at this moment. Rankings are updated every hour, so if I check back later in the day, the sales rank will likely be different. For practical purposes, a single Amazon sales rank will tell you very little about the overall sales performance of a book. On its own, the Amazon sales rank is pretty useless, but sales rank data that is compiled over time, can tell us a lot. When the rankings are tracked, compiled, and averaged every hour for days, weeks, months, and years, we can start to make informed assumptions about a book's performance.

The Amazon rank becomes meaningful when it is tracked long enough to show how well a book has sold against other books over the course of several months rather than for just one hour. Using Amazon data, book-tracking websites like RankForest.com and TitleZ.com track and compile the sales ranks over extended periods. For example, Titlez.com will show the current rank of any title on Amazon, as well as seven, thirty, and ninety-day rolling averages, and a *lifetime* average performance of a book.

Based on the top one million books, one can conclude that a title with a lifetime average rank of 150,000 or better has performed in the top 15% of book sales on Amazon. If you want to know how a book is performing, take its lifetime average on Titlez.com (or other book-tracking website) and divide by one million to get the percentage. For example, the chess book we examined earlier has a *lifetime* average (which happens to be eight months) of 5896. We can conclude that for the past eight months, *Practical Chess Exercises* has averaged in the top 5.8% of book sales on Amazon. If I compared it to all five million titles on Amazon, the percentage would be more impressive but as explained earlier, less meaningful.

This approach is not without its flaws, but it is the most accurate method available to measure the success of books and the firms who publish them. When a book has averaged in the top 15% for several months, or even years, you should consider it a success. For a better idea of actual sales numbers, consider the following Nielsen BookScan statistics.

- Of the 1.2 million titles tracked by BookScan each year, the average book sells 500 copies.
- Those in the top 2% sell over 5000 copies per year.
- Those in the top 4% sell over 1000 copies per year.

Achieving Success

Success in writing involves a lot of hard work and determination. You don't have to be a prolific writer or a marketing guru to succeed. You just have to embrace the business side of writing by producing a quality book, writing in a profitable genre, and using smart marketing strategies. Your writing doesn't have to be groundbreaking to be successful. It just needs to be valuable to a specific group of people, your market.

If you have a book inside you waiting to be written, or if you have written a book and are waiting to be published, I urge you to move forward confidently into self-publishing. The next chapter looks at hundreds of successful titles recently published by the firms in this book.

Authors of both fiction and non-fiction have found success through self-publishing. Some have several books selling consistently in the top 15%. Many have become best sellers and all of them have earned higher royalty payments than they would have through conventional publishing. Based on long-term Amazon rankings, the titles in the next chapter prove that self-published authors do succeed, that self-published books can compete, and that done well, they can outshine conventionally published titles.

2
Nonfiction Success

To illustrate how possible it is to find success with a self-publishing firm from this book, hundreds of their current books are listed in this chapter. These are books that are selling in the top 15% on Amazon. The titles will not only give you confidence that self-publishing works, they will also give you an idea of the variety of titles that sell well in the non-fiction, self-published market. Provided in order are the title, author, publishing firm, and performance of each book. These are all current titles sustaining sales at the top of the market—some of them for several years running.

Though it is impossible to know the precise sales results for a book, when the performance is tracked for several months or years, as is the case here, the numbers closely reflect the success achieved. The following titles prove that success in self-publishing is not just chance and that the results are repeatable. (For an explanation of how these titles have been tracked, review pages 5 and 6.)

HCG Weight Loss Cure Guide
Linda Prinster, CreateSpace. Amazon Bestseller.

How to be a Super Hot Woman
Mandy Simons, Outskirts. Selling in the top 1%.

Not Manifesting? This Book is for You!
Kathleen Mackenzie, Outskirts. Selling in the top 2%.

If I'm So Smart, Why Can't I Lose Weight?
Brooke Castillo, BookSurge. Selling in the top 2%.

Practical Chess Exercises: 600 Lessons from Tactics to Strategy
Ray Cheng, Wheatmark. Top 1% for more than two years.

The AdSense Code: What Google Never Told You About Making Money with AdSense
Joel Comm, Morgan James. New York Times Bestseller.

Raw Foods for Busy People, Jordan Maerin, Lulu. Top 1% for over four years.

Wire Wrapping: The Basics and Beyond (jewelry making)
Jim McIntosh, CreateSpace. Selling in the top 1% for over a year.

The Big Book Of NLP Techniques
Shlomo Vaknin, BookSurge. Selling in the top 1%.

We Married Koreans
Gloria Goodwin Hurh, Llumina Press. Selling in the top 1%.

Football Outsiders Almanac 2009: The Essential Guide to the 2009 NFL and College Football Seasons
Aaron Schatz, CreateSpace. Selling in the top 1%.

Outrageous Advertising That's Outrageously Successful
Bill Glazer, Morgan James. Top 1%.

How to REALLY use LinkedIn
Jan Vermeiren, BookSurge. Top 1%.

BlackBerry Tour 9600 Made Simple
Martin Trautschold, BookSurge. Top 1%.

Runner Life 2009-2010: The RUSH-A Handbook
Matthew Woodman, CreateSpace. Top 1%.

Pocket Guide to the HCG Protocol
Tiffany Prinster, CreateSpace. Top 1%.

The 5-Minute Plantar Fasciitis Solution
Jim Johnson, Dog Ear. Top 1%.

The Spunky Coconut Cookbook: Gluten Free, Casein Free, Sugar Free
Kelly V. Brozyna, BookSurge. Selling in the top 2%.

Etsy Exposed: 50 Ways to Start Making More Etsy Sales Than You Can Handle
Jessica Schope, CreateSpace. Selling in the top 2%.

Sominology: Learn Sleep Medicine in One Weekend
Teofilo Lee-Chiong, CreateSpace. Selling in the top 2%.

Garden Haiku: Raising Your Child with Ancient Wisdom
Lily Wang, iUniverse. Top 2%.

BlackBerry® 8800 & 8300 Curve Made Simple
Martin Trautschold, BookSurge. Top 2%.

Math SAT 800: How To Master the Toughest Problems
Dan Eiblum MSEd, BookSurge. Top 2%.

Attracting Abundance with EFT: Emotional Freedom Techniques
Carol Look (currently has two books selling in the top 12%), AuthorHouse. Selling in the top 9%.

Better Than Steroids (fitness book)
Dr. Warren Willey, Trafford. Selling in the top 3% for over a year.

Leadership and Training for the Fight
Paul R. Howe, AuthorHouse. Top 1% for over two years. Author currently has two books performing in the top 2%.

Yoga Posture Adjustments and Assisting
Stephanie Pappas, Trafford. Top 2% for three years.

Antichrist: Islam's Awaited Messiah
Joel Richardson, Pleasant Word. Top 2% for three years.

The Zen of Meeting Women: First and Second Editions
Max Weiss, CreateSpace. Both books selling in the top 13%.

How I Made My First Million on the Internet and How You Can Too!
Ewen Chia, Morgan James. Top 2%.

My HCG Tracker: A Motivational and Inspirational Companion for the HCG Protocol
Tiffany Prinster, CreateSpace. Top 2%.

Lose the Weight Caused by Antidepressants
James L Harper, CreateSpace. Top 2%.

SEO Made Simple: Strategies For Dominating The World's Largest Search Engine
Mr. Michael H. Fleischner, CreateSpace. Selling in the top 3%.

The Potty Boot Camp: Basic Training For Toddlers
Suzanne Riffel, Booklocker. Top 3%.

The Lyme Disease Solution
Kenneth B. Singleton M.D., BookSurge. Top 3%.

Competition BBQ Secrets: A Barbecue Instruction Manual for Serious Competitors and Back Yard Cooks Too
Bill Anderson, BookSurge. Selling in the top 4%.

The Miracle Mineral Supplement of the 21st Century 3rd edition
Dr. Jim Humble, BookSurge. Selling in the top 4%.

Michael Jackson Conspiracy
Aphrodite Jones, iUniverse. Selling in the top 4%.

Cold Water Crossing: An Account of the Murders at the Isles of Shoals
David Faxon, CreateSpace. Selling in the top 4%.

Trading Stock Options
Brian Burns, CreateSpace. Selling in the top 4%.

Mastering Search Advertising: How the Top 3%. of Search Advertisers Dominate Google AdWords
Rich Stokes, iUniverse. Selling in the top 4%.

What Your Mother Never Told You: A Teenage Girls Survival Guide
Richard Dudum, BookSurge. Selling in top 8% for two years.

7-Slide Solution(tm): Telling Your Business Story In 7 Slides or Less

Paul J. Kelly, BookSurge. Selling in the top 5% for over a year.

My Stroke of Insight: A Brain Scientist's Personal Journey

Jill Bolte Taylor, Lulu. Author sold rights to Viking Publishing and book was featured on Oprah's radio show.

Options Trading 101

Bill Johnson, Morgan James. Top 7% for over a year.

The Life of Your Dreams in 30 Days or Less!

Cindy Day, iUniverse. Selling in the top 12% for over a year.

The 45 Second Presentation That Will Change Your Life

Don Failla, AuthorHouse. Top 3% for over three years.

Slow and Steady Get Me Ready (activities for children)

June Oberlander, Xulon. Top 2% since 2004.

The Fundamentals of Listing and Selling Commercial Real Estate

Loren Keim, Infinity. Selling in the top 3%.

The Sixty-Second Motivator

Jim Johnson (also the author of *Treat Your Own Rotator Cuff*), Dog Ear. Top 2% for three years.

Beyond Positive Thinking

Robert Anthony, Morgan James. Top 3% since 2005.

Treat Your Own Rotator Cuff

Jim Johnson, Dog Ear. Top 1% for over two years.

WORD: A Real Dog Locked in a Shelter Cage for Eight Years

Florence Petheram, Pleasant Word. Top 6% for over a year.

Death to Diabetes (causes and management of type two diabetes)

DeWayne McCulley, BookSurge. Top 4% for over two years.

What to Eat with IBD

Tracie M. Dalessandro, iUniverse. Picked up by CMG Publishing.

Sell Your Book on Amazon

Brent Sampson, Outskirts. Top 2% for over two years.

101 Worry Free HCG Diet Recipes
Linda Prinster, CreateSpace. Amazon Bestseller.

Starting Your Career as a Wall Street Quant
Brett Jiu, Outskirts. Top 6% for two years.

Successful QuickBooks Consulting
Michelle L. Long, CreateSpace. Top 3% for over a year.

From Zero to Hero: How to Master the Art of Selling Cars
Jeffrey Knott, iUniverse. Top 6% for over a year.

How to Dominate $1 and $2 No Limit Hold 'Em
Sam O'Connor, AuthorHouse. Top 11% for over two years.

First Aid for the Betrayed (dealing with adultery)
Richard Alan, Trafford. Published in 2006 and still selling in the top 4%.

Islam and Terrorism: What the Quran Really Teaches About Christianity, Violence and the Goals of the Islamic Jihad
Mark A. Gabriel, Creation House. Top 4% for over five years.

Those Crazy Germans! A Lighthearted Guide to Germany
Steven Somers, Xlibris. Top 4% for over a year.

How to Study in Medical School
Armin Kamyab, AuthorHouse. Top 4%.

The Goddess of Raw Foods
Nwenna Kai, BookSurge. Selling in the top 5%.

The Furniture Wars: How America Lost a 50 Billion Dollar Industry
Michael K. Dugan, BookSurge. Selling in the top 5%.

Caw of the Wild: Observations from the Secret World of Crows
Barb Kirpluk, iUniverse. Published in 2005 and still selling in the top 5%.

Pray, Hope, and Don't Worry: True Stories of Padre Pio
Diane Allen, Aventine. Selling in the top 5%.

What To Do When You Become The Boss
Bob Selden, Outskirts Press. Top 5%.

Exit Strategies for Covered Call Writing: Making the most money when selling stock options
Alan Ellman, Wheatmark. Top 5%.

Java/J2EE Job Interview Companion - 400+ Questions & Answers
A. Kumaraswamipillai, Lulu. Top 6% for over a year.

Official SAT Study Guide Solutions Manual: 2007-2008 Edition
Van Tsai, CreateSpace. Selling in the top 6%.

Sometimes a Woman Needs a Horse (a personal story)
Betsy Talcott Kelleher, Pleasant Word. Top 5% for more than three years.

The Final Theory: Rethinking Our Scientific Legacy
Mark McCutcheon, Universal Publishers. Still in top 6% after being published in 2004.

A Year In the Life of an ESL (English Second Language) Student
Edward J. Francis, Trafford. Published in 2004 and still selling in the top 3%.

Four Steps To Building A Profitable Coaching Practice
Deborah Brown-Volkman, iUniverse. Top 3% for more than five years.

Laparoscopic Adjustable Gastric Banding
Jessie H. Ahroni, iUniverse. Top 5% for over five years.

Light Infantry Tactics: For Small Teams
Christopher E. Larsen, AuthorHouse. Top 3% for three years.

Why Doesn't My Doctor Know This?
David Dahlman, Morgan James. Selling in the top 10%.

Cancer-Free: Your Guide to Gentle, Non-toxic Healing
Bill Hendersen (currently has two books in the top 13%), BookLocker. Top 2% for over a year.

How to Write and Publish Your Own eBook in as Little as 7 Days
Jim Edwards, Morgan James. Top 5% for over two years.

Nearly Normal Cooking For Gluten-Free Eating
Jules Shepard, BookSurge. Top 5% for over two years.
Sophie-Safe Cooking (recipes free of common food allergies)
Emily Hendrix, Lulu. Top 3% for two years.
Grimorium Verum (extra-terrestrials)
Joseph H. Peterson, CreateSpace. Top 5%.
The Havanese (dog care)
Diane Klumb and Joanne Baldwin, BookSurge. Top 5% for over a year.
How to Become an Alpha Male
John Alexander, Lulu. Top 3% for four years.
My Husband's Affair Became the Best Thing That Ever Happened to Me
Anne Bercht, Trafford. Top 3% for four years.
The Easiest Way to Meet and Pick up Girls...Ever!!
Dusty White, BookSurge. Top 7% for over three years.
Indigo Adults: Forerunners of the New Civilization
Kabir Jaffe, iUniverse. Top 5% for three years.
365 Deployment Days: A Wife's Survival Story
Sara Dewalt, BookPros. Top 7% for over a year.
Guitar Electronics Understanding Wiring and Diagrams
T.A. Swike, CreateSpace. Top 5% for over a year.
Profit from Prices: All You Need for Profit in Stock Trading is Stock Prices
Jayesh Patel, CreateSpace. Top 14% for over a year; earning up to $14 a book.
Everything You Need to Know About House Training Puppies & Adult Dogs
Lori Verni, Lulu. Published in 2005 and still in the top 5%.
It's Not About the Weight: Attacking Eating Disorders from the Inside Out
Susan J. Mendelsohn, iUniverse. Top 7% for over two years.
Mexico City: An Opinionated Guide for the Curious Traveler
Jim Johnston, iUniverse. Top 14% for over a year.

The Great Cholesterol Con (new perspectives on high cholesterol)
  Anthony Colpo, Lulu. Top 6% for over two years.
In Fitness And In Health
  Dr. Philip Maffetone, BookSurge. Selling in the top 6%.
Satan's Dirty Little Secret
  Steve Foss, Creation House. Selling in the top 6%.
The Seven Mountain Prophecy
  Johnny Enlow, Creation House. Selling in the top 6%.
BlackBerry® Storm 9500 Made Simple
  Gary Mazo, BookSurge. Top 6%.
Compelling Conversations: Questions and Quotations on Timeless Topics- An Engaging ESL Textbook for Advanced Students
  Eric H. Roth, BookSurge. Top 6% for over two years.
Americans' Survival Guide to Australia and Australian-American Dictionary
  Rusty Geller, Virtual Bookworm. Top 6%.
Foundations of IT Service Management
  Brady Orand, BookSurge Top 6%.
The Portrait Photographers Posing Guide: How to Pose People for Portraits
  Nigel Holmes, BookSurge. Top 12%.
The Ever-Transcending Spirit (metaphysical)
  Toru Sato, iUniverse. Top 6% since 2003.
Spiritual Marketing: A Proven 5-Step Formula for Easily Creating Wealth from the Inside Out
  Joe Vitale, AuthorHouse. Top 8% for seven years.
Almost Home: My Life Story
  Damien Echols, iUniverse. Top 7% for over five years.
Appreciative Team Building: Positive Questions to Bring Out the Best of Your Team
  Diana Whitney, iUniverse. Top 4% for over four years.

Leadership Coaching: The Disciplines, Skills, and Heart of a Christian Coach
Tony Stoltzfus, BookSurge. Selling in the top 5%.

RAW in Ten Minutes (eating raw foods for health)
Bryan Au, Trafford. Top 7% for over three years.

Servicing ITIL: A Handbook of IT Services for ITIL Managers and Practitioners
Randy A. Steinberg, Trafford. Selling in the top 10%.

The Reiki Teacher's Manual: A Guide for Teachers, Students and Practitioners
Tina Zion, AuthorHouse. Selling in the top 7%.

The Craft of Tattooing
Erick Alayon, BookSurge. Top 7%.

Click Here to Order: Stories of the World's Most Successful Internet Marketing Entrepreneurs
Joel Comm, Morgan James. Top 7%.

Get Out Of Our House: Revolution! (A New Plan for Selecting Representatives)
Tim Cox, BookPros. Selling in the top 8%.

The Eye of Revelation: The Ancient Tibetan Rites of Rejuvenation
Peter Kelder, Booklocker. Top 8%.

The Spiritual Formation of Leaders
Chuck Miller, Xulon Press. Top 8%.

The Game Inventor's Guidebook: How to Invent and Sell Board Games, Card Games, Role-Playing Games, & Everything in Between!
Brian Tinsman, Morgan James. Top 8%.

The Official SAT Study Guide Solutions Manual
Van Tsai, CreateSpace. Top 8%.

Every Man Sees You Naked: An Insider's Guide to How Men Think
David M. Matthews, Wheatmark. Top 8%.

Channel Surfing: Riding the Waves of Channels to Profitable Trading
Michael Parsons, AuthorHouse. Published in 2005 and still selling in the top 9%.

The Rules of Engagement: Binding the Strongman
N. Cindy Trimm (has two books through this publisher in the top 5%), Creation House. Top 5% for over two years.

The Plain Truth about Living in Mexico
Doug Bower, Universal Publishers. Top 7% for over four years.

Every Rescued Dog has a Tale
Deborah Eades, Lulu. Top 9% for over a year.

Female Domination
Elise Sutton, Lulu. Top 7% for over five years.

The Enabler: When Helping Hurts the Ones You Love
Angelyn Miller, Wheatmark. Published in 2001 and still selling in the top 4%.

Lean Project Management: Eight Principles For Success
Lawrence Leach, BookSurge. Top 9%.

MySpace Music Profit Monster (online marketing strategies)
Nicky Kalliongis, BookSurge. Picked up by MTV Press.

Raw and Radiant: Simple Raw Recipes for the Busy Lifestyle
Mary Rydman, Outskirts. Top 5% for over a year.

The School Psychology Licensure Exam Guide
Peter Thompson, iUniverse. Top 5% over four years.

Your Healing Diet: A Quick Guide to Reversing Psoriasis and Chronic Diseases with Healing Foods
Deirdre Earls, BookSurge. Top 9% for over two years. Book can also be found in Whole Foods grocery stores.

Improve Your Eyesight with EFT
Carol Look, AuthorHouse. Selling in the top 9%.

Track Your Plaque (heart disease prevention)
William R. Davis, iUniverse. Top 5% for four years.

Raising a Vaccine Free Child
   Wendy Lydall, AuthorHouse. Top 7% for over three years.
Intense Minds: Through the Eyes of Young People with Bipolar Disorder
   Tracy Anglada, Trafford. Top 7% for over two years.
Speaking Better French
   Saul H. Rosenthal, Wheatmark. Selling in the top 7%.
Meat Smoking and Smokehouse Design
   Stanley Marianski, Outskirts. Top 4% for over two years.
Building Tomorrow's Talent: A Practitioner's Guide to Talent Management and Succession Planning
   Doris Sims and Mathew Gay, AuthorHouse. Top 10%.
A Trader on Wall Street: A Short Term Traders Guide
   Michael Coval, iUniverse. Top 12% for seven years.
How to Get SSI & Social Security Disability
   Mike Davis, iUniverse. Published in 2000 and still selling in the top 6%.
Revenge of Killer Sudoku (A book of puzzles)
   Djape, Lulu. Top 8%.
Drive Without Fear: The Insecure Driver's Guide to Independence
   Norman Klein, AuthorHouse. Published in 2000 and still selling in the top 9%.
The Fine Print of Self-Publishing, Second Edition
   Mark Levine, Mill City. Top 5% for over two years.
Writing for Emotional Impact
   Karl Iglesias, WingSpan. Top 7% for four years.
Questions and Answers on Life Insurance
   Anthony Steuer, iUniverse. Top 10% for over a year.
The Second Great Depression
   Warren Brussee, BookLocker. Top 10% for more than four years.
Freezer Bag Cooking: Trail Food Made Simple
   Sarah Svien Kirkconnell, Lulu. Top 6% for over two years.

Planting Design Illustrated
Gang Chen, Outskirts. Selling in the top 12% for over a year.

The Official Student Doctor Network Medical School Admissions Guide
Christian Becker, Mill City Press. Top 9% for over a year.

Awol on the Appalachian Trail
David Miller, WingSpan. Top 6% for over two years.

Basic Counseling Techniques: First and Second Editions
C. Wayne Perry, AuthorHouse. Both selling in the top 12%.

Child Custody A to Z: Winning with Evidence
Guy J. White, iUniverse. Top 7% for over three years.

Rome with Kids: An Insider's Guide
J.M. Pasquesi, BookPros. Top 6% for over two years. Outperforming Fodor's *Around Rome with Kids.*

Get the Skinny on Silver Investing
David Morgan, Morgan James. Top 10% for three years.

Adkisson's Captive Insurance Companies
Jay D Adkisson, iUniverse. Top 9% for two years.

Becoming a Police Officer: An Insider's Guide to a Career in Law Enforcement
Barry M. Baker, iUniverse. Top 6% for over two years.

Living The Secret Everyday
Joanne Scaglione and Suzanne Stitz, BookSurge. Top 7%.

Nine Days in Heaven: The Vision of Marietta Davis
Dennis Prince and Nolene Prince, Creation House. Top 10%.

The Russian Adoption Handbook: How to Adopt from Russia, Ukraine, Kazakhstan, Bulgaria, Belarus, Georgia, Azerbaijan and Moldova
John H. Maclean, iUniverse. Top 10% for over five years.

Teach Your Child the Multiplication Tables
Eugenia Francis, Infinity. Top 8% for over two years.

Opinion Writing 2nd Edition
Ruggero J. Aldisert, AuthorHouse. Top 9%.

Devils and Demons and the Return of the Nephilim
John Klein, Xulon. Published in 2005 and still selling in the top 9%.

The Official Student Doctor Network Medical School Admissions Guide
Christian Becker, Mill City Press. Top 9%.

Managing Life with Kids: Simple Solutions to Organize Your Family and Home
Mary Caroline Walker, BookSurge. Top 9%.

100 Tips for Hoteliers: What Every Successful Hotel Professional Needs to Know and Do
Peter Venison, iUniverse. Top 9%.

Today's Homestead: Volume I
Dona Grant, Virtual Bookworm. Selling in the top 10%.

Nine Days in Heaven: The Vision of Marietta Davis
Dennis Prince, Creation House. Selling in the top 10%.

The Stronghold of God
Francis Frangipane, Creation House. Selling in the top 10% for over five years.

The Political Campaign Desk Reference: A Guide for Campaign Managers and Candidates Running for Elected Office
Michael McNamara, Outskirts. Top 11%.

The Road Gets Better From Here
Adrian Scott, Virtual Bookworm. Top 11%.

State Secrets: An Insider's Chronicle of the Russian Chemical Weapons Program
Vil S Mirzayanov, Outskirts. Top 11%.

Cars and People: How to Put the Two Together (auto sales)
Ziegler, iUniverse. Top 11% for five years.

Special Needs Trust Administration Manual: A Guide for Trustees
Barbara D Jackins, iUniverse. Top 8% for over four years.

Everything the Instructors Never Told You About Mogul Skiing
Dan DiPiro, AuthorHouse. Top 12% for two years.

Certain to Win (military strategies applied to business)
Chet Richards, Xlibris. Top 10% for five years.

Learning to Be Me: My Twenty-Three-Year Battle with Bulimia
Jocelyn Golden, iUniverse. Top 11% for over two years.

Self-Change Hypnosis
Richard MacKenzie, Trafford. Top 8% for four years.

The Client's Guide to Cognitive-Behavioral Therapy
Aldo R. Pucci, iUniverse. Top 6% for over a year.

Breaking into the Art World: How to Start Making a Living As an Artist
Brian Marshall White, VirtualBookworm. Top 12% for over three years.

Advanced Lucid Dreaming - The Power of Supplements
Thomas Yuschak, Lulu. Selling in the top 8%.

The Gangs of Los Angeles (true crime)
William Dunn, iUniverse. Top 9% for over two years.

Realities of Foreign Service Life: Volumes One and Two
Patricia Linderman, iUniverse. Both in the top 10%.

Fidget to Focus: Outwit Your Boredom: Sensory Strategies for Living with ADD
Roland Rotz, iUniverse. Published in 2005, and still selling in the top 12%.

Our Troth: History and Lore
Kveldulf Gundarsson, BookSurge. Top 11% for over a year, earning $9 a book.

Biblical Nonsense: A Review of the Bible for Doubting Christians
Jason Long, iUniverse. Top 13%.

Discovering Denali
Dow Scoggins, iUniverse. Top 9% for over four years.

Preferred Stock Investing
  Doug K Le Du, BookLocker. Top 15%.
An Applicant's Guide to Physician Assistant School and Practice
  Erin L. Sherer, CreateSpace. Top 8%.
Malignant Medical Myths
  Joel M. Kauffman, Infinity. Top 12% for over two years.
Tournament Poker
  Mitchell Cogert, CreateSpace. Selling in the top 5%.
Play Razz Poker to Win
  Mitchell Cogert, CreateSpace. Selling in the top 13%.
The Pre-Dental Guide: A Guide for Successfully Getting into Dental School
  Joseph S. Kim, iUniverse. Published in 2001 and selling in the top 7%.
Everything You Will Ever Need To Know To Start Driving A Big Truck Or How I Became A Professional Tourist
  Steve Richards, Outskirts. Top 13% for over two years.
Stuff Good Players Should Know: Intelligent Basketball from A to Z
  Dick Devenzio, BookPros. Top 9% for over two years.
F1rst Guide for the College Placement Test (CPT)
  Rachel Goldberg, iUniverse. Selling in the top 12%.
Living and Retiring in Hawaii
  James R. Smith, iUniverse. Top 12% for over five years.
MATLAB Advanced GUI Development
  Scott T. Smith, Dog Ear. Top 12% for over two years.
Six Disciplines for Excellence (small business development)
  Gary Harpst, BookPros. Top 9% for over two years.
Sense and Goodness Without God
  Richard Carrier, AuthorHouse. Selling in the top 11% for two years.
The Business Startup Checklist and Planning Guide
  Stephanie Chandler, Aventine. Top 12% for four years.

The Maui CEO: Import from China, Sell on eBay, and Live Wherever You Want
John Tennant, iUniverse. Top 14%.

The Sensitive Person's Survival Guide
Kyra Mesich, iUniverse. Published in 2000 and still selling in the top 11%.

Americans' Survival Guide to Australia and Australian-American Dictionary
Rusty Geller, Virtual Bookworm. Selling in the top 6% for over a year.

Midlife Mavericks: Women Reinventing their Lives in Mexico
Karen Blue, Universal Publishers. Published in 2000 and still selling in the top 13%.

A Daughter's Worth: A Bible Study for Teenaged Girls
Ava Sturgeon, Tate. Top 11%.

Marketing 2.0: Bridging the Gap between Seller and Buyer through Social Media Marketing
Bernie Borges, Wheatmark. Selling in the top 12%.

How to Attract Money Using Mind Power
James, Infinity. Selling in the top 12%.

Writing About Art
Marjorie Munsterberg, CreateSpace. Selling in the top 12%.

Young and Revolting: The Continental Journals of Nick

Gloom to Glory: Trials and Tribulations of a True Philly Sports Fan
Dan Nolan, Outskirts Press. Top 12%.

Clean House, Strong House
Kimberly Daniels, Creation House. Top 12%.

Shooting the Stickbow
Anthony Camera, Virtual Bookworm. Top 12%.

A Happy Pocket Full of Money
David Cameron Gikandi, Xlibris. Top 13%.

Mind Your Diet
Dr. Melinda Blackman, Xlibris. Top 13%.

Psalm 91
  Peggy Joyce Ruth, Creation House. Top 13%.

Eric is Winning (his story of surviving Lou Gehrig's disease)
  Eric Edney, Xlibris Top 10% for over three years.

The Culture of Critique: An Evolutionary Analysis of Jewish Involvement in Twentieth-Century Intellectual and Political Movements
  Kevin MacDonald, AuthorHouse. Published in 2002 and still selling in the top 12%.

Dances With Marmots - A Pacific Crest Trail Adventure
  George G. Spearing, Lulu. Selling in the top 10%.

Life After Gastric Bypass
  Gerald Wayne, AuthorHouse. Selling in the top 8%.

Constitution Translated for Kids
  Cathy Travis, BookPros. Top 11% for over two years.

Counseling Survivors of Sexual Abuse
  Diane Langberg, Xulon. Published in 2003 and still selling in the top 11%.

Head for Mexico: The Renegade Guide
  Don Adams, Trafford. Top 15% for over five years.

Measuring ITIL
  Randy A. Steinberg (has two books in the top 11%),
  Trafford. Top 6% for over two years.

The Ancient Hebrew Lexicon of the Bible
  Jeff A. Benner, Virtual Bookworm. Top 11% for over four years.

Learn to Read Biblical Hebrew
  Jeff A. Benner, Virtual Bookworm. Published in 2004 and still in the top 14%.

Ultrarunning: My Story
  Mike Bouscaren, BookSurge. Selling in the top 12%.

Devil Dog Diary: A Day by Day Account of US Marine Corps Training
  GYSGT Will Price, Outskirts. Selling in the top 10%.

Renewable Energy Policy
  Paul Komor, iUniverse. Published in 2004 and selling in the top 10%.

Fundamental Spanish
  Barbara Bregstein, Trafford. Top 9% for over two years.

Classroom Blogging
  David Warlick, Lulu. Selling in the top 14%.

Our Troth: Living the Troth
  Kveldulf Gundarsson (has three self-published books selling in the top 14%), BookSurge. Top 14%.

Guerrilla Marketing for Financial Advisors
  Grant Hicks and Jay Conrad Levinson, BookSurge. Top 14% for more than five years.

More Easy Beans: Quick and Tasty Bean, Pea and Lentil Recipes
  Trish Ross, BookSurge. Top 11%.

Staying in Alignment: Life in the Higher Realms Series
  Karen Bishop, BookLocker. Top 15%.

An Introduction To Enterprise Architecture
  Scott A. Bernard, AuthorHouse. Top 12%.

Chasing The Gender Dream
  Jennifer Merrill Thompson, Aventine. Selling in the top 15%.

What All Little Girls Need & What Most Women Never Had
  Joe Cucchiara, Tate. Selling in the top 13%.

Auto Accident Personal Injury Insurance Claim
  Dan Baldyga, AuthorHouse. Published in 2001 and still selling in the top 15%.

I'm Still Your Mother: How to Get Along with Your Grown-Up Children for the Rest of Your Life
  Jane Adams, iUniverse. Published in 2001 and still selling in the top 12%.

Incorporate & Get Rich!: How to Cut Taxes 70% & Protect Your Assets Forever!
  C.W. Allen, BookSurge. Selling in the top 14%.

The Mathematics of Relativity for the Rest of Us
Dr. Louis Jagerman M.D, Trafford. Selling in the top 14%.

The Breast Stays Put: No Chemo-No Radiation-No Lumpectomy-No Thank You
Pamela Hoeppner, Xulon Press. Selling in the top 14%.

Knowing Pains: Women on Love, Sex and Work in our 40s
Molly Tracy Rosen, WingSpan. Selling in the top 14%.

Student Organization Leadership: A Guide for Student Leaders
Cyrus Fakharzadeh, Aventine. Top 15%.

The Happy Minimalist
Peter Lawrence, Xlibris. Top 15%.

Cure Your Cancer
Bill Henderson, AuthorHouse. Top 13% for six years.

Good Food in Mexico City: A Guide to Food Stalls, Fondas and Fine Dining
Nicholas Gilman, iUniverse. Top 14%.

Eden: The Knowledge of Good and Evil 666
Joye Jeffries Pugh, Tate. Top 12%.

Research Strategies: Finding your Way through the Information Fog
William B. Badke, iUniverse. Top 9%.

Language Processing Problems: A Guide for Parents & Teachers
Cindy Gaulin, Xlibris. Published in 2000 and still in the top 14%.

Puberty Survival Guide for Girls
Dr. Eve Anne Ashby, iUniverse. Top 13% for over four years.

3
Fiction Success

The odds for success don't exactly favor fiction, so if you choose to write in this genre be prepared for the challenge. Of the self-published books selling at the top of the market, fewer than 15% are fiction. Nonetheless, the titles below prove that self-published fiction books can prevail, and several authors here demonstrate that one successful book can lead to a successful series.

Just as the case for the nonfiction titles, it is impossible to know the precise sales results for a book. However, when the Amazon sales performance is tracked for several months or years, as is the case here, the numbers closely reflect the success achieved. Complete book descriptions can be found on Amazon.com and publisher websites. (For an explanation of how these titles have been tracked, please review pages 5 and 6.)

Patriots: Surviving the Coming Collapse: A Novel of the Turbulent Near Future
James Wesley Rawles, Xlibris. Published over three years ago and remains an Amazon bestseller.

The Orphaned Anything's
Stephen Christian, iUniverse. Selling in the top 6%.

As The World Dies: Siege: A Zombie Trilogy
Rhiannon Frater, CreateSpace. Top 1%.

As The World Dies: Fighting To Survive: A Zombie Trilogy
Rhiannon Frater, CreateSpace. Top 3%.

As The World Dies: The First Days: A Zombie Trilogy
Rhiannon Frater, CreateSpace. Top 2%.

A Marriage Worth Earning: To Have and to Hold
Mary L. Sherwood, CreateSpace. Selling in the top 2%.

Uncommon Emotions
Lynn Galli, Outskirts Press. Selling in the top 2%. Author has four novels published through Outskirts all selling in the top 7% or better.

Still Alice
Lisa Genova, iUniverse. Selling in the top 2%.

Something Like Regret
Kara Louise, Lulu. Selling in the top 3%.

In Jupiter's Shadow
Gregory Gerard, Infinity. Selling in the top 9%.

Kevin Knows the Rules: Introduces Classroom Rules To Kindergarten Through Third Grade Students
Molly Dowd, AuthorHouse. Top 3%.

Connelly's Flame
Aliyah Burke, Lulu. Selling in the top 9%.

A Little Bit Psychic
Aimee Avery, CreateSpace. Selling in the top 3%.

A Lover's Regret: The Ramseys
AlTonya Washington, iUniverse. Selling in the top 11% for over a year.

Double Bound
Nick Nolan, BookSurge. Selling in the top 8%.

Strings Attached
Nick Nolan, BookSurge. Selling in the top 3% for over three years.

Accidental Slave
Claire Thompson, BookSurge. Selling in the top 4%.

Darcy's Dreams
Regina Jeffers, Xlibris. Top 10%.

Darcy's Passions
Regina Jeffers, Xlibris. Top 15%.

Monster Hunter International
Larry Correia, Infinity. Selling in the top 3%.

Soldier of Rome: The Sacrovir Revolt
James Mace, iUniverse. Top 9%.

Soldier of Rome: The Legionary: A Novel of the Twentieth Legion during the Campaigns of Germanicus Caesar
James Mace, iUniverse. Top 12%.

Leadville
James D. Best, Wheatmark. Selling in the top 7%.

Torpedo
Jeff Edwards, iUniverse. Selling in the top 8% for over three years.

Revoltingly Young
C.D. Payne, Infinity. Top 15%.

Secretary's Punishment
J.W. McKenna, BookSurge. Top 3%.

Suffer in Silence
David Reid, Virtual Bookworm. Top 6% for over four years.

She Slipped and Fell
Shonda, AuthorHouse. Selling in the top 3%.

Sweet Farts (children's book)
Raymond Bean, BookSurge. Top 1%.

In Search of Rhett Butler
Sharron Haynes, iUniverse. Published over four years ago, and still selling in the top 15%.

The Trials of the Honorable F. Darcy
Sara Angelini, Lulu. Selling in the top 2%.

Vengeance Is Mine
Brandy Purdy, iUniverse. Top 3%.

The Binky Ba-ba Fairy (children's)
Heather Knickerbocker, Dog Ear. Top 15%.

Assumed Engagement
Kara Louise, Lulu. Selling in the top 6%.

Code Name Honey Pot
Keith Wander, BookSurge. Top 7%.

Brandon And The Bipolar Bear: A Story For Children With Bipolar Disorder
Tracy Anglada (two books in the top 7% for over two years), Trafford. Top 7%.

Wasted Heart
Lynn Galli, Outskirts Press. Top 6% for nearly three years.

The Big One
Stuart Slade, Lulu. Top 15%.

Trolling Nights
Savannah J. Frierson, Lulu. Selling in the top 12%.

TwiLite: A Parody
Stephen Jenner, Virtual Bookworm. Top 4%.

Unloveable Bitch
Allysha Hamber, CreateSpace. Top 3%.

Imagining Reality
Lynn Galli, Outskirts Press. Top 7%.

Blessed Twice
Lynn Galli, Outskirts Press. Selling in the top 6%.

Grandfather's Tale: The Tale of a German Sniper
Timothy Erenberger, iUniverse. Published in 2001 and still selling in the top 10%.

The Traitor's Wife: A Novel of the Reign of Edward II
Susan Higginbotham, iUniverse. Top 8% for nearly two years.

A Wish In Time
  Laurel Bradley, iUniverse. Top 12% for nearly three years.
Letters to Erik: The Ghost's Love Story
  An Wallace, Outskirts Press. Top 15%.
The Mouse Who Lived at Fenway Park (children's)
  Bradford James Nolan, AuthorHouse. Selling in the top 4%.
Pemberley's Promise
  Kara Louise, Lulu. Top 10%.
Slave of the Legion
  Marshall S Thomas, BookLocker. Top 10%.
Anvil of Necessity
  Stuart Slade, Lulu. Top 10%.
The Shopkeeper
  James D. Best, Wheatmark. Top 8% for two years.
The Shut Mouth Society
  James D. Best, Wheatmark. Top 8%.
Threads
  Nell Gavin, Infinity. Top 13%.
Rise and Walk
  Gregory Solis, Lulu. Top 11% for over a year.
When The Bronx Burned
  John J Finucane, iUniverse. Selling in the top 13%.
Who Are My Real Parents?
  D. L. Fuller, CreateSpace. Selling in the top 13%.
The Pict
  Jack Dixon, iUniverse. Top 14%.
Private Entrance
  Kathryn Harvey, iUniverse. Top 15%.

4
Publishing Packages

Self-publishing offers you the opportunity to scrutinize, compare, contrast, and ultimately select the company best suited for you and your book. The cost of publishing and the royalties you receive are important, but they should not be the only deciding factors. Before you can make an informed decision, you need to know what to look for in a publisher, how to pinpoint the crucial elements in a publishing contract, where it's okay to splurge, and how to avoid unnecessary costs.

Most firms offer a choice of publishing packages that include a variety of services for a flat fee. The best packages include everything you need to publish and sell your book and nothing more. What you pay for publishing should be in line with the services offered, the royalties paid, and the sales performance of the firm.

In the interest of higher profits, publishers often encourage writers to upgrade their initial publishing packages. Unless you can prove the extra cost will come back to you in sales, stick to the packages recommended in this book. Most upgraded selections are overpriced and don't generate enough additional sales to offset the added expense. The publisher profiles in this book always recommend the package of greatest value.

The successes of several reasonably priced companies demonstrate that you don't have to spend a fortune to publish a top selling book. Avoid spending money on useless perks, and instead, look at how each firm addresses these twelve components of publishing:

- Sales Results
- Formatting
- Binding
- Cover Design
- Distribution
- Trade Discounts
- Retail Royalties
- Publisher Website Royalties
- Timeline
- Book Pricing
- Author Purchase Discounts
- Author Rights and Contract

Sales Results

If their books don't sell, it doesn't matter if a publisher pays great royalties or has excellent distribution. Because sales performance is critical for success, every firm profiled is here because they have a track record of book sales. Surprisingly, sales performance doesn't always correlate as expected with the cost of publishing. Some of the lowest priced firms actually generate the some best sales results. Additionally, don't assume that a more expensive company offers better quality. If they don't sell as many books, the quality they claim to offer doesn't mean anything.

Formatting

Your manuscript will need to be converted to a PDF and formatted for printing in a book. Unless otherwise noted, all packages recommended include PDF conversion and book formatting. The process of formatting a book into a print ready PDF is very simple and takes only a few minutes. Most companies offer formatting for free, so be wary of any firm that charges more than $50 for this service.

Binding

Bookstore quality paperbacks are bound with a method called Perfect Binding, which is used by all of the firms profiled here. The majority of companies offer hard cover binding as well, but I don't recommend it if you're looking to make money. As lovely as hard cover books can be, they are very expensive to produce and that cost will be taken directly out of your royalty payments, often reducing royalties to pennies per book. For that reason, the recommended publishing packages for each firm will be for paperback Perfect Binding.

Cover Design

If your firm doesn't include cover design in the publishing package, find out what their cover templates look like and how much flexibility you will have with colors. You should also do a search on Amazon (click on Advanced Search) to glance over their covers. Most of the templates from publishers in this book look just as good as the custom designed covers. Some publishers require you to supply your own cover art for your book. Avoid creating a cover on your own unless you have experience in graphic design and a basic understanding of how to use software for designing covers.

Distribution

Each publisher in this book has access to a variety of distribution channels. Some firms offer only limited access while others have expansive relationships with multiple distributors. The biggest bookstore distributors in the U.S. are Ingram and Baker & Taylor, but the most important sales channel for a self-published book is registration with Amazon.com. The overwhelming majority of self-published authors will tell you they see more sales through Amazon than through any other single bookseller, online or otherwise.

As you review the directory of firm profiles, you will notice that sometimes a firm with excellent distribution has below average sales results or that a firm with limited distribution has excellent sales results. When faced with a choice, *always choose strong sales over great distribution*. After all, your royalty checks will be driven by your book sales.

Below are the six main components of distribution.
- ISBN
- Bar Code
- Books in Print
- Wholesalers (Ingram and Baker & Taylor)
- Registration with online booksellers
- LCCN

ISBN (International Standard Book Number)

A unique International Standard Book Number, or ISBN, is assigned to each book on the market and is used all over the world to identify a book for libraries and booksellers. Think of it as a social security number for your book. If you don't already have your own unique ISBN number, your publisher will assign one to your book. Each version (hardback, paperback, electronic, etc) and edition of your book will be assigned a different ISBN. If your publisher assigns your ISBN and you decide to leave that publisher to pursue another firm, a new ISBN will be assigned to your book by the new publisher.

Bar Code

Required by wholesalers and retailers, a bar code is used to scan the price of your book at the cash register. Your publisher will assign a bar code and print it on the back cover of your book.

Books in Print

The largest independent book database is Bowker's Books in Print. Registration with Books in Print is not required, but it makes it easy for anyone who wants to stock your book to find it.

Wholesalers

Instead of ordering thousands of individual titles from each publisher, retailers order books through wholesalers and have them shipped directly to their stores. Ingram is the number one wholesaler in the book industry. Baker & Taylor is the second. Your publisher will likely have a relationship with one or both of them. Access to one of these wholesales is required for access to brick and mortar bookstores. Without Ingram or Baker & Taylor, your book has zero chance of landing on the bookshelves of a major bookstore.

Online Registration

Your publisher will register your book with Amazon.com and other online booksellers such as Barnes & Noble, Abe Books, and Borders to make it available for online purchases. As previously mentioned, Amazon.com will likely be your strongest source of sales, making this distribution channel an absolute must for self-publishers.

LCCN (Library of Congress Control Number)

Libraries require this number to order books. Though it's not required (most of my own books don't have an LCCN), libraries do have large budgets for ordering new books each year. If you've written a book that you think libraries may be interested in, it's worth your while to get an LCCN assigned to it. If your firm does not assign an LCCN, ask them for one. It's free and easy to acquire.

Trade Discounts

The trade discount is the amount of money reduced from the retail price of your book to arrive at a wholesale price for retailers. The difference between the retail price and the wholesale price (or discount) is where bookstores make their money.

Some publishers set a fixed discount for all retailers while others give the author freedom to set discounts as they see fit. Anything lower than a 55% discount will prevent your book from being stocked regularly on bookstore shelves, but a 30%-40% discount will make your book available for special order upon request. The discount required by Amazon ranges from 20-55% depending on the publisher.

Trade discounts are important to consider because they will directly affect your sales as well as your bottom line. A discount of only 20% will mean more money in your pocket, but also that brick and mortar bookstores will never stock your book. Your sales will come exclusively from online retailers.

A large discount, say 55%, will encourage bookstores to stock your book but will eat sharply into your royalties. The key is to strike a balance and know where you most want to derive book sales. A happy medium is a 30-40% discount that still offers room for decent royalties and makes your book available upon customer request at bookstores. In the end, it's up to you and your own specific goals.

Discounts are often dismissed or overlooked by new authors because they either don't understand them or they don't know how significant discounts are to success. As you read about each company, I invite you to pay close attention to the discounts they use.

Royalties

Royalty payments are one of the most significant factors in choosing a publisher. Unfortunately it can also be one of the most confusing and misleading areas of self-publishing. When researching royalties always look at the actual dollar amount you will receive rather than the percentage paid.

An 80% royalty can be half as much money in your pocket as a 50% royalty, depending on *how much is deducted* before the percentage is calculated. Each firm calculates royalties differently, so when you see 30% royalties advertised, your first question should always be, "30% of what?" Most companies pay a percentage of the retail price minus the trade discount and the cost to print the book (production cost).

The example below shows one way in which an 80% royalty looks after the production cost and discount are deducted.

Retail Price of the Book:	$14.95
Minus 40% Discount for Retailers:	-$5.98
Minus Production Cost:	-$4.80
Profit remaining:	**$4.17**
80% Royalty on $4.17:	**$3.34**

Because every firm charges a different production cost, two firms that pay an 80% royalty won't necessarily pay the same dollar amount once the calculations are complete. Below is an example of the how different production costs can have surprising outcomes for the same book.

Royalty	Retail Price	Discount	Pro-duction Costs	Profit Remaining	Author Income
100%	$14.95	40%	$6.70	$2.27	$2.27
80%	$14.95	40%	$5.90	$3.07	$2.46
50%	$14.95	40%	$4.50	$4.47	$2.24
40%	$14.95	40%	$2.80	$6.17	$2.47

As you can see, the royalty percentage doesn't even give you a ballpark idea of how much you will be paid. Notice that the publisher with the lowest royalty rate actually pays the highest dollar amount. This example is typical of what you will find in the industry. As a rule, high advertised royalties usually mean higher production costs and lower author incomes. Don't be fooled by the percentages. Let the actual dollar amounts be your guide.

Differences in page count will affect the prices in different ways for each firm, so always contact a company you're considering to request a royalty quote for the real dollar amount (*not* the percentage) you can expect to make on each sale, based on the dimensions and page count of your book.

Royalties from Publisher Website

Some publishers allow customers to buy books directly through their websites to avoid the retail discount that stores require. If you are connected to a group of people inclined to buy your book, encourage them to buy from you or your publisher directly, for maximum profit.

You will often find high royalty rates advertised on publisher websites only to find later that the rate applies exclusively to books sold through their site. In most cases, only a small percentage of books, if any, are sold through the publisher directly. The most important royalty rates are those earned through big booksellers.

You will be paid differently for books sold on the firm's website than you will for bookstore sales or for books sold through online retailers like Amazon. Be sure to obtain quotes for books sold through each retail channel. When you are quoted from your publisher, find out if the quote is for books sold through their website or elsewhere. Stay away from any company reluctant to provide you with specific information, even if it is a firm named in this book.

Timeline

Depending on the package you choose and any extra services you request, the timeline for turning your manuscript into a book will vary. If you add copyediting or opt for a custom cover design, expect to wait longer for completion. Turn-around times range from one week to six months.

Book Pricing

Firms either set the price of your book without your input or allow you to control the pricing. Either way, take care to ensure that your book price will be competitive with other books in its genre. The price of your book will impact the amount of money you earn as well as the number of people likely to buy it. A book priced considerably higher than the competition will scare away buyers if the price is not justified.

Author Purchases

Most firms allow authors to purchase copies of their own books at a discount. If you plan to send out a lot of review copies or expect to have speaking engagements, run seminars, or sell a significant number of books through channels other than traditional retail, pay close attention to author purchase prices.

Author Rights and Contract

Not all publishers give authors the same book rights. If you are confident that your how-to book will never play on the big screen, movie rights can be overlooked; but what about the rights to your book itself?

Some firms give all rights to you and make it easy to cancel your contract. They give you complete control and ask for nothing in return. Other publishers claim all the rights to your book once you sign on the dotted line and retain those rights to prevent you from ever using another publisher.

Lean toward companies that offer you the greatest ownership of your material and that make it easy to cancel your contract. When you pay money to have your book published, it makes sense to remain in control of your material.

For more about contracts, read the most recent edition of *The Fine Print of Self Publishing* by Mark Levine. An experienced attorney, Levine translates into plain words the real meaning of phrases and contract terminology.

Additional Services Available

Most firms offer an array of add-on services, from editing to marketing, that you can choose after you've selected a publishing package. Before adding on a bunch of extras, make sure you will see a return on your investment in the form of book sales. Don't feel pressured by sales people and do shop outside your publisher for competitive prices. You will often find less expensive alternatives on your own. Though many other unnecessary extras are available, listed next are the only add-ons you'll need for a successful book.

Professional editing is one of the most important things you can do to prepare your book to sell in high volumes. Editing is not included in most publishing packages, so you should either find an outside source to edit your book or pay your publisher for the service. Under no circumstances should you edit your own work.

The marketing services offered by self-publishers are not always a good value for the money. Promotional efforts often include a poorly written and poorly executed press release, a website, and a pile of posters and bookmarks (which won't sell your book). Outside companies can often do website hosting and press releases more effectively for less money. See chapter nine for more on promoting your book.

Custom cover design is a service worth looking into. The cover of your book will be a deciding factor for many people who buy it. Most of the publishers offer cover templates in their packages that work just fine, but if you want something unique, consider paying the extra money to have your cover created by a professional.

Submitting a Manuscript

Since the last update, many of these firms have begun a submission process that asks authors to submit a manuscript, and a day or so later the firms "accept" it. I suppose the idea is to give authors some feeling of *getting published*, but the reality is, self-publishing firms accept all manuscripts, which is the point of self-publishing in the first place. So, you shouldn't be intimidated about submitting a manuscript for "approval," nor should you be overjoyed when it is "accepted."

5
Analyzing the Firms

Every publisher has its strengths and weaknesses and with twenty-two top performers to choose from, you are sure to find the right fit. Key deciding factors and offerings are listed for each firm along with hard numbers for costs and royalty payments. The information is broken down into easy-to-read profiles that can be used for direct comparison between companies. After reading through the profiles, you can use the chart at the end of chapter six to narrow down your search. Each publisher is rated on several criteria, including:

- Sales Results
- Recommended Publishing Packages
- Amazon Royalties
- Bookstore Royalties
- Distribution
- Author Purchases
- Overall Value

Sales Results
★★★★★ These firms have the highest rate of books selling in the top 15%.

★★★★ These firms see strong book sales.

★★★ Not the top performers but may make sense for specific author needs.

★★ These are companies that show potential but have yet to prove themselves with consistently strong sales.

Best Publishing Package
This price refers to the cost of the best-value publishing package offered and is the one recommended in the firm profile. Recommendations favor packages with the best distribution and the fewest number of unnecessary extras.

Amazon Royalties
The dollar amount listed represents how much the author is paid for each book sold on Amazon. The number is based on a 150-page book that retails for $14.95, unless otherwise noted.

Bookstore Royalties
This dollar amount represents how much the author is paid for each book sold at brick and mortar bookstores. Numbers are based on a 150-page book selling for $14.95.

Distribution
★★★★★ Listing with Ingram *and* Baker & Taylor, and registration at Amazon.com and other online retailers.

★★★★ Listing with either Ingram *or* Baker & Taylor and registration at Amazon.com and other online retailers.

★★★ Registration only at Amazon and other online retailers.

Author Purchases
The quoted price is for author purchased copies of the book, direct from the publisher, and represents the cost per book for a bulk order of 250 copies. Prices are based on a 150-page book that retails for $14.95.

Overall Rating

The overall rating takes into account the combination of publishing costs, offerings in the package, sales performance, and royalty payments.

Excellent - These are the crème of the crop. They deliver outstanding service and products at a very competitive price. Strongly recommended.

Good - These firms offer a great service in exchange for the price they charge. They also pay well and have a solid record of book sales.

Average - These firms do a decent job of everything but either fail to shine in any particular area or have weaknesses that outweigh their strengths. Firms with this rating should be considered a good choice when they fill specific needs that higher rated firms cannot.

Not recommended - When a firm falls into this category, it is usually because they have a history of shady practices or because the cost of publishing far outweighs the benefits they offer.

Disclaimer

The numbers in the chart and in the company profiles are based on information available at the time of publication. Some dollar amounts are estimates, and all numbers should be verified with the publisher before moving forward. All prices are subject to change at the discretion of the publisher.

6
Top Self Publishing Firms

After years of analysis and observation, the following twenty-two firms have made the cut for the 2010 update. They were chosen for the sales performance of their books in the market place and examined for what they offer in terms of value, royalties, distribution, and other features including the trade discounts and the author agreement.

The firms are listed in alphabetical order. Each profile includes the contact information, distribution, and elements included in the packages, add-on services offered by the firm, and everything else you need to make an informed choice about a self-publisher. For each firm, you will see a *Best Publishing Package.* This is the package that offers the most value for the money and doesn't include unnecessary extras that drive the cost up.

At the end of this chapter, on page 112, is a handy comparison chart of all the firms so that you can see how each company stacks up, head to head. Though these companies do not alter their prices or policies often, it is always possible that something has changed, so be sure to confirm numbers and costs directly with a company before moving forward with them.

AuthorHouse

SNAPSHOT

Overall Rating: Good

Royalties: Average

Sales Results: ★ ★ ★ ★

Distribution: ★ ★ ★ ★ ★

AuthorHouse is one of several self-publishers owned by parent company Author Solutions. It is independently maintained and operated and sets its own policies.

Contact Info

AuthorHouse
1663 Liberty Drive, # 200
Bloomington, IN 47403

www.AuthorHouse.com
Email through website
1-888-519-5121

Best Publishing Package

The Foundation Package for $599 includes custom cover design, interior layout design, ebook formatting, and one copy of your book. Full color interior publishing available for $1299. These packages also include:

- ISBN
- Bar Code
- Wholesalers – Ingram and Baker & Taylor
- Website Listings - Amazon.com, Barnes&Noble.com, Borders.com

Services Available

Copyediting, custom illustrations, design, promotion, marketing, and expedited service. For $699 you can add bookstore returns.

Trade Discounts

A 40% discount is extended to retailers, which means your book will be available for special order at brick-and-mortar stores.

Timeline

Up to six months. An extra $500 ensures a thirty-day turn around.

Retail Royalties

A 150-page book priced at $14.95 will pay up to15% royalty, or $2.24. For more information on royalties, go to **www.AuthorHouse.com/GetPublished/BookSales.aspx**

Royalties through Publisher Website

Between 5% and 50% depending your book price.

Book Pricing

AuthorHouse sets a minimum price, which you can adjust.

Author Purchases

A 150-page book costs about $7.00 per copy.

Author Rights and Contract

If you cancel your contract, AuthorHouse can legally retain the full rights to your book and prevent you from changing firms. AuthorHouse has removed their main contract from the website, but you can still find a few of their contracts at the end of the order forms at: **www.authorhouse.com/OrderAgreement.aspx**

Strength

- $599 is a great price for excellent distribution and custom cover design.

- Book sales have improved significantly in the past year.

Weaknesses
- Author purchased books are expensive.
- Contract can be impossible to break.

Conclusion
The $599 publishing package and strong distribution are great features, and the company's sales results are stronger than ever. This is a solid firm with years of experience.

Aventine Press

SNAPSHOT
Overall Rating: Excellent   **Royalties:** Average
Sales Results: ★★★★   **Distribution:** ★★★★

Contact Info
Aventine Press
750 State St. #319
San Diego, CA 92101

AventinePress.com
info@AventinePress.com
1-866-246-6142

Best Publishing Package
Aventine charges $399 for interior templates, two copies of your book, indexing of up to twenty-five words, inclusion of author photo and biography for back cover. Custom cover design runs $295, templates are $175. Package includes:
- ISBN

- Bar Code
- Wholesalers - Ingram
- Website Listings - Amazon.com, Barnes&Noble.com, BooksaMillion.com, Buy.com

Services Available

Competitively priced copy editing, custom cover design, image scanning, and color image insertions.

Trade Discounts: A 55% discount is given to all retailers which will encourage bookstores to stock your book.

Timeline: About three months.

Retail Royalties

Eighty percent of the retail price minus production cost and discount. A $14.95 book sold on Amazon or at any bookstore will pay $2.68 in royalties.

Book Pricing

Aventine sets the book price—$12.95 for a 150-page book. They have stated that they are willing to adjust a book's price upon special request from the author.

Author Purchases

Production cost plus 10%, which is $3.47 for a 150-page book.

Author Rights and Contract

Author retains book rights. Aventine allows easy exit of the contract. Worth noting is Aventine's easy to read and easy to access (via their website) contract, that proves they have nothing to hide.

Strengths

- Proven track record of strong sales.
- Aventine extends deep discounts to retailers without compromising your royalties. This is rare in the industry and worth considering.
- Transparency and favorable contract terms.
- Great prices for author purchased books.

Conclusion

One of the long-standing favorites, Aventine offers a great value and a solid track record of sales. Even though royalties are somewhat average, Aventine remains an excellent value because the trade discount they offer to retailers is so high. Aventine is a great choice for writers who are serious about brick-and-mortar bookstore sales. A 55% discount will encourage bookstores to stock your book and will allow Amazon to offer it at a reduced price to customers (which will help your Amazon sales).

BookLocker

SNAPSHOT

Overall Rating: Good

Sales Results: ★ ★ ★ ★

Royalties: Average

Distribution: ★ ★ ★ ★

Contact Info

BookLocker.com, Inc.
PO Box 2399
Bangor, ME 04402

www.BookLocker.com
Email through website

Best Publishing Package

BookLocker charges $299, which includes publishing services and eBook formatting. Cover design is $200 additional, $150 for a template. Color interior books are available for $317 plus $5.50 per page, plus $6.50 per image. (A 90 page full color book will cost well over $1000. Annual hosting fee is $18.00. Packages include:

- ISBN
- Bar Code
- Wholesalers – Ingram
- Website Listings - Amazon.com, Barnes&Noble.com, and other online retailers

Services Available

Limited editing support and marketing programs.

Trade Discounts

BookLocker sets a 30% discount, which means your book will not be stocked on bookstore shelves, but it will be available for special order upon request.

Timeline: Six weeks.

Retail Royalties

Fifteen percent of the list price, regardless of production cost or discounts. A $14.95 book will pay $2.24.

Royalties through Publisher Website

Thirty-five percent of the list price for print books and 50%-70% of the list price for eBooks.

Book Pricing

They set the minimum list price—$13.95 for a 150-page book. Authors can increase it from there.

Author Purchases
Discounts start at 35% off the list price and increase with volume orders.

Author Rights and Contract
Author retains full book rights. BookLocker makes it easy to cancel the contract.

Noteworthy
Returning authors pay only $149 for the publishing package to publish subsequent titles.

Strengths
- The publishing package is an exceptional value that includes wide distribution, flexible book pricing, and decent royalties.
- Strong track record of book sales.

Weakness
- Book Locker's website is not up to modern standards. On the upside, they have been very responsive to email.
- Author purchased copies are among the most expensive in the industry.
- Cost for full color publishing is very high.
- Through the years of updating this book, BookLocker is a company I've received multiple complaints about. The complaints have never been about quality or timeliness, but consistently refer to less than polite customer service representatives.

Conclusion
BookLocker offers a solid record of sales and very low publishing costs without compromising the quality of the product. On the downside, their website is not up to current

standards and they do not offer phone support. If you are comfortable with email only communication, (and willing to put up with potentially rude responses) BookLocker delivers a decent value for the price.

BookPros

SNAPSHOT

Overall Rating: Not Recommended

Royalties: Excellent

Sales Results: ★ ★ ★ ★ ★

Distribution: ★ ★ ★ ★ ★

Contact Info

BookPros
2100 Kramer Lane, #300
Austin, TX 78758

www.BookPros.com
Info@BookPros.com
1-512- 478-2028

Best Publishing Package

Total costs start at $13,000 and include editing, printing, layout, custom cover design, marketing and promotion, Amazon Search Inside, Google Book Search, copyright registration, a press kit, two press releases, and an author bio. BookPros also requires authors to purchase 1200 books, which adds at least $4800 to the bill.

- ISBN
- Bar Code
- Books in Print
- LCCN
- Wholesalers – Ingram and Baker & Taylor

- Website Listings - Amazon.com, Barnes&Noble.com, and more

Services Available
Multiple levels of editing, advanced marketing, and promotion.

Trade Discounts: Usually 50%-55%.

Timeline: Ten to eighteen months.

Retail Royalties
Authors receive 40-45% of the retail price, regardless of production cost or discounts. A 150-page book selling for $14.95 pays about $6.15 for sales on Amazon and other bookstores.

Author Purchases
Production cost plus 15%. A 200-page book will cost around $4.40. Costs decline as volume increases.

Author Rights and Contract
You retain the rights to all of your materials. BookPros makes it easy to cancel the contract.

Strengths
- The highest royalties in the industry, even with a 55% discount to retailers. Very impressive.
- Excellent prices for author purchased books.
- Deep discounts to retailers.
- Excellent sales results.

Weaknesses

- At $17,800, you should have a very good reason for choosing this firm. At $6.15 a book in royalties, you will need to sell nearly 3000 copies just to break even on your publishing fees. That means your book will have to sell consistently in the top 1-2% of the market for this firm to make sense.
- Authors are stuck with a personal purchase of 1200 books to store and try to personally sell or give away.
- Though much is included in this package, the timeline should be considerably shorter.

Conclusion

Even with excellent sales results and the highest royalties in the industry, BookPros is not one I can recommend. Huge financial sacrifices and required author purchases make no sense in a world of print-on-demand publishing. Unless you have a great justification for it, avoid any publisher that seeks to part you with this much money.

BookSurge Publishing

SNAPSHOT

Merged with CreateSpace: See next page

Owned by Amazon.com, BookSurge has been absorbed by another Amazon owned self-publisher, CreateSpace.com. While BookSurge has been a major player in the self-publishing world, and historically recommended by previous editions of this book, Amazon assured writers that they will receive the same services and benefits previously offered through BookSurge, but with the higher royalty payments offered by CreateSpace. Because CreateSpace is a favorite of mine, I don't have any complaints or warnings about this merger. In fact, the strengths of the two companies should combine to create a powerful combination for self-publishing.

CreateSpace

SNAPSHOT

Overall Rating: Excellent   **Amazon Royalties:** Excellent

Sales Results: ★ ★ ★ ★ ★   **Distribution:** ★ ★ ★ ★ ★

CreateSpace, owned by Amazon.com, has merged with BookSurge (another Amazon owned company) to provide more author support and distribution than has been available in the past.

CreateSpace previously required authors to create their own cover art and format their own manuscripts. This worked great for experienced professionals because of the cost savings, but fell short for everyone else. Now CreateSpace offers a broader spectrum of customer support, while still offering more experienced writers the opportunity to do it themselves and publish for free.

Contact Info

CreateSpace Receiving   www.CreateSpace.com

100 Enterprise Way, # A200   Info@CreateSpace.com

Scotts Valley, CA 95066

Best Publishing Package

The Pro Plan for $39 gets you a choice of cover templates, the Search Inside feature on Amazon.com and the option to submit your own ISBN and use your own imprint. (Recommended for those who can create a cover and convert a manuscript to PDF) Full color publishing is also available. Package includes:

- ISBN

- Bar Code
- Expanded Distribution to reach bookstores, online retailers, libraries, and academic institutions
- Website Listing with Amazon.com

Services Available

CreateSpace now offers design and formatting packages that start at $299 and go up to packages that include everything from editing to press releases for $2586. Services can be purchased ala carte as well. Custom cover design starts at $299.

Timeline

Once you submit your cover and manuscript, the turnaround time is just a few days (sometimes a few hours!). CreateSpace will send you a proof of your book to approve before listing it for sale. If you are not satisfied with the proof, you can make as many changes as needed, for no additional cost.

Retail Royalties

CreateSpace keeps 40% of the list price as well as the cost of production and gives you the balance. A 150-page book selling for $14.95 will pay $6.32 in royalties at Amazon, and $3.33 through brick and mortar stores. A 150-page full color book priced at $29.95 will pay $6.62 in royalties. Go to **www.createspace.com/Products/Book/** for a calculator.

Royalties through Publisher Website

Same as Retail Royalties, except CreateSpace keeps only 20% of the list price instead of 40%. The example above would pay $9.31 through the CreateSpace website.

Book Pricing: You control the pricing.

Author Purchases

The $39 package allows authors to purchase books for $0.85 plus $0.012 per page, which is $2.65 for a 150-page book. Full color interior books are $0.07 per page plus $0.85, or $11.35 for a 150 page book.

Author Rights and Contract

Authors retain full rights to their material. CreateSpace makes it easy to cancel the author contract.

Noteworthy

CreateSpace is the only reputable self-publisher in the industry to provide a FREE option for book publishing. The package includes an ISBN, Amazon.com distribution, and somewhat lower royalty payments than other options.

Strengths

- Very high Amazon.com book sales.
- Among the highest royalty payments in the industry.
- Fastest turnaround time in the industry.
- Lowest cost publisher in the industry.
- Best prices for author purchased books in the industry.
- Highest royalties and lowest production costs for full color books.

Weaknesses

- CreateSpace offers the greatest value to those who are able to convert material to PDFs and create cover art on their own.
- At present, the website does not make it easy to find information on the expanded publishing packages (you can find it in the FAQ section).

Conclusion

At $39, CreateSpace is by far, the lowest price publisher out there. The low cost of publishing and high royalties combined with very strong Amazon sales more than make up for other shortcomings. If you or someone you know can convert your book to a PDF and design a cover, you can make as much money in royalties as you would with any other publisher (or more), for a much lower price. For many writers CreateSpace is a fantastic value.

Creation House Press

SNAPSHOT

Overall Rating: Not Recommended   **Royalties:** Poor

Sales Results: ★ ★ ★ ★   **Distribution:** ★ ★ ★ ★

Contact Info

Strang Book Group   www.CreationHouse.com
600 Rinehart Rd.   Email through website
Lake Mary, FL 32746

Best Publishing Package

Creation House charges no publishing fee but requires a large, upfront purchase of books. The last quote was a minimum purchase of 2000 books for an out of pocket cost of $22,400. Publishing services include cover design, custom interior layout, copyright registration, limited marketing efforts, proofreading, and multiple levels of editing. Included are:

- ISBN
- Bar Code
- Books in Print - No
- LCCN
- Wholesalers - Baker & Taylor
- Website Listings - Amazon.com and other online retailers

Services Available
Advertising, marketing, and warehousing.

Trade Discounts: Unclear

Timeline: About four months.

Retail Royalties
Five percent of the retail price, regardless of production cost and discounts. A $14.95 book will pay .75 cents in royalties.

Royalties through Publisher Website
Twelve percent of the retail price.

Book Pricing: You control the pricing.

Author Purchases
Twenty-five percent discount on 2000 copies, which is $11.20 for a $14.95 book.

Strength
- Excellent sales results.

Weaknesses
- The upfront cost is unacceptable in today's self-publishing world.

- Unusually high prices for author purchased books.
- Royalties are among the lowest in the industry.

Conclusion

Creation House made the list, in spite of the unnecessarily large upfront investment, because their books sell so well in the market. They may be one of the top performing self-publishing firms, but their business strategy, very low royalties, and out of pocket cost of $22,000 make them a poor choice overall.

Dog Ear

SNAPSHOT

Overall Rating: Excellent	Royalties: Excellent
Sales Results: ★ ★ ★ ★ ★	Distribution: ★ ★ ★ ★ ★

Contact Info

Dog Ear Publishing
4010 West 86th St. # H
Indianapolis, IN 46268

www.DogEarPublishing.net
Helpme@DogEarPublishing.net
1-866-823-9613

Best Publishing Package

The Basic Package for $1099 includes custom cover design, interior layout, and five copies of your book, a webpage, up to thirty images or five tables, and submission to the Google Book Search program. Full color interior publishing is also available with this package. Package includes:

- ISBN
- Bar Code
- Books in Print
- LCCN
- Wholesalers – Ingram and Baker & Taylor
- Website Listings - Amazon.com and other major online retailers

Services Available
Editing, marketing, expedited service for $500, and bookstore returns for $200.

Trade Discounts
You can set average or aggressive discounts.

Timeline: Two to eight weeks.

Retail Royalties
One-hundred percent of the retail price minus production cost and discounts. A 150-page book sold for $14.95 (with a 40% discount) on Amazon or at any bookstore will pay you $4.69.

Book Pricing: You set the price.

Author Purchases
Cost is $1.28 per book plus $0.02 per page. A 150-page book will cost you $4.28. Offset printing is available for quantities over 2000, which further reduces cost.

Author Rights and Contract
Author retains rights to all book materials. Dog Ear makes it easy to cancel the contract.

Strengths

- Dog Ear pays some of the highest royalties in the industry.
- Great prices for author purchased books including offset printing.
- Excellent distribution.
- Dog Ear allows authors the flexibility to offer deep discounts to retailers for no additional cost or binding contract agreement.

Weakness

- Though Dog Ear offers many features in their Basic Package, the cost of publishing with them is high.. For authors that don't require a website, who have no images in their books, and who can do their own submission to Google Book Search, Dog Ear may not be the best choice.

Conclusion

Dog Ear is an outstanding self-publisher. Though their packages are on the pricey side, they receive an excellent rating in every category measured by this book.

Foremost Press

SNAPSHOT
Overall Rating: Good

Royalties: Average

Sales Results: ★ ★ ★

Distribution: ★ ★ ★ ★ ★

Contact Info
Foremost Press
7067 Cedar Creek Rd.
Cedarburg, WI 53012

www.foremostpress.com
email through website
1-262-377-3180

Best Publishing Package
Plan A for $347 is a good value that includes a light spelling and grammar edit, interior layout, and ten copies of your book. Cover design in $150 extra. Package includes:
- ISBN
- Bar Code
- Wholesalers – Ingram and Baker & Taylor
- Website Listings - Amazon.com, BarnesAndNoble.com

Services Available
Editing and custom cover design.

Trade Discounts
Unclear.

Timeline: Two to eight weeks.

Retail Royalties
Twenty percent of the retail price. A 150-page book sold for $11.97 on Amazon will pay $2.39. Brick and mortar bookstore

sales pay 50% of the profit (after discounts and printing charges are deducted).

Book Pricing: Foremost sets the price. A 150 page book sells for a reasonable price tag of $11.97.

Author Purchases
Authors receive a discount of 50% off the retail price for book purchases. Minimum order is ten copies.

Author Rights and Contract
Author retains rights to all book materials. Foremost makes it easy to cancel the contract.

Noteworthy
Though Foremost uses Lightning Source for printing (which will print books in a variety of dimensions), Foremost allows authors to print only 6x9 inch books. While this is the most common size and shouldn't cause a problem for most writers, it can certainly be a limitation for certain types of books.

Strengths
- Foremost doesn't attempt to confuse customers with complicated offerings or contracts. They make self-publishing very simple and straightforward—the way it should be.
- Excellent distribution.

Weakness
- Foremost does not offer cover design or cover templates in any of their packages. The $150 extra for cover design is through a referral, not in house work at Foremost.

- Pricing for author purchased copies is on the high end of the spectrum.

Conclusion

Foremost Press has been an up and comer over the past few years and has finally earned a spot in this book among the other top publishing companies. It is a bit too early to say they have a solid track record of book sales, but they're looking good so far. I look forward to seeing more great things from them in the future.

Infinity Publishing

SNAPSHOT

Overall Rating: Good

Sales Results: ★ ★ ★ ★

Royalties: Average

Distribution: ★ ★ ★ ★ ★

Contact Info

Infinity Publishing
1094 New Dehaven St, # 100
W. Conshohocken, PA 19428

www.InfinityPublishing.com
Email through website
1-877-289-2665

Best Publishing Package

Infinity charges $499 for a package that includes bookstore returns and custom cover design. Package also includes:
- ISBN
- Bar Code
- Books in Print

- Wholesalers - Baker & Taylor (additional $149 to add Ingram)
- Website Listings - Amazon.com, Borders.com, Booksamillion.com, (Barnes&Noble.com included in the $149 addition for Ingram)

Services Available

Editing, marketing, and Ingram distribution. Infinity also offers a program called "CD in a Book" that encloses a CD for customers in each copy sold. Ebook formatting is also available.

Trade Discounts

Infinity extends a 40% discount to all retailers, which means your book will not be presented on bookstores shelves, but it will be available by special order upon customer request.

Retail Royalties

Fifteen percent of the sales price, regardless of production cost or discounts. A 150-page book selling for $14.95 will pay $2.24 in royalties.

Royalties through Publisher Website

Thirty percent of the selling price.

Book Pricing: You control the pricing.

Author Purchases

Authors receive 40-50% off the list price plus a 10% royalty payment.

Author Rights and Contract

Author retains full book rights. Infinity makes it easy to cancel the contract.

Strengths

- Their publishing package is an outstanding value at $499 that includes custom cover design and bookstore returns.
- The "CD in a Book" program is a great feature not offered by other firms.
- For an additional $149, you have the flexibility to expand your distribution to include Ingram and registration with Barnes&Noble.com.

Conclusion

Infinity is a solid company with a great publishing package that includes custom cover design. Their book sales have improved over previous years, they pay fair royalties, and offer expanded distribution for a fair price.

iUniverse

SNAPSHOT

Overall Rating: Average	**Royalties:** Below Average
Sales Results: ★ ★ ★ ★ ★	**Distribution:** ★ ★ ★ ★ ★

With over 35,000 unique titles published, iUniverse is a giant in the self-publishing industry. Owned by parent company Author Solutions, iUniverse is independently maintained and operated.

Contact Info:

iUniverse, Inc.
1663 Liberty Drive, # 300
Bloomington, IN 47403

www.iUniverse.com
Email through website
1-800-AUTHORS

Best Publishing Package

The Select Package for $599 includes custom cover design, book design and layout, one free round of author proof corrections, five copies of your book, up to 25 black and white image insertions, a page on publisher's website, and eBook formatting. $25 annual fee. Package includes:

- ISBN
- Bar Code
- Wholesalers - Ingram and Baker & Taylor
- Website Listings - Amazon.com, Barnes&Noble.com, BooksaMillion.com, and more

Services Available

Editing, marketing, indexing, custom cover design, proof reading, copyright registration, bookstore returns, and ghostwriting.

Trade Discounts

Automatic 36% discount to retailers. This means at brick-and-mortar bookstores, your book will be available for special order upon customer request and will not be stocked on the shelves. For a fee of $99, you can opt for a 50% discount and a 10% royalty. If you decide to select this option, iUniverse will not allow you to switch back later.

Timeline: 45-120 days

Retail Royalties

Twenty percent of the retail price after shipping, tax, discounts, and returns are deducted. A rough estimation shows a $14.95 book sold on Amazon, or any bookstore paying around $1.91 in royalties. If you opt for the 50% discount, your royalties will be reduced to ten percent, and payment would be $0.96.

Royalties through Publisher Website

Same as Retail Royalties.

Book Pricing

iUniverse sets the price, $14.95 for 150-page book.

Author Purchases

Authors receive 30%-60% off the retail price, depending on volume. An order of 250 books receives a 50% discount.

Additional Programs

iUniverse offers a program for special events such as book signings or seminars. The retailer or organization where the event takes place can order your book ahead of time at 45% off the retail price and you will receive royalty payments on the books ordered.

Author Rights and Contract

Authors retain book rights, and iUniverse allows authors to terminate the contract after three years, with a 30-day written notice.

Once an author signs up for the 50% discount / 10% royalties program, they are bound to that program and cannot switch back to the original one. This means that if your book doesn't sell any better with the deeper discount, you will not have the option to reverse your decision and go back to a higher royalty payment. Think carefully before choosing this option.

Strengths

- Highly experienced publisher with a solid record of book sales.
- The $599 publishing package is a great value that includes custom cover design and excellent distribution.

Weaknesses

- Below average royalty payments. When you consider that iUniverse offers only a 36% discount to stores, they have plenty of money left over to pay a higher royalty to authors, but they pocket that money instead.
- iUniverse allows authors to offer 50% trade discounts to retailers for an extra $99 and a reduced royalty payment of 10%, usually considered a strong point because it encourages bookstores to stock a book. However, they don't allow you to change your decision later on, and because the majority of your sales will not come from bookstores, you run the risk of having a permanently reduced royalty percentage.

Conclusion

Despite strong sales and a reasonable publishing package, iUniverse misses the mark with below average royalties. They make up for their lack in pay with strong sales, but because they are being outdone by competitors in their price range, both in pay and in features, they received a rating of average. Once a top choice for writers, iUniverse has lost some its shine.

Llumina Press

SNAPSHOT

Overall Rating: Not Recommended
Sales Results: ★ ★ ★

Royalties: Poor
Distribution: ★ ★ ★ ★ ★

Contact Info

Llumina Press
7915 W. McNab Road
Tamarac, FL 33321

www.Llumina.com
Deborah@Llumina.com
1-866-229-9244

Best Publishing Package

The Trade Paperback Package for $799 includes basic cover design, back cover edit, interior formatting, ten free books, and a page on the publisher's website. Full color publishing is also available in this package. The Ready-to-Go Package, for $299, works well for folks who can format their own PDF's and create their own covers. Other features of both packages include:

- ISBN
- Bar Code
- Books in Print
- LCCN
- Wholesalers - Ingram and Baker & Taylor
- Website Listings - Amazon.com, Barnes&Noble.com, and more

Services Available

Bookstore returns, ebook formatting, expedited service for $499, marketing, and editing.

Trade Discounts: Llumina allows you to set your own discount.

Retail Royalties
Ten percent of the list price, regardless of production cost and discounts. A 150-page book will retail for $13.95 and pay $1.40 in royalties for all sales channels.

Royalties through Publisher Website
Thirty percent of the list price.

Book Pricing
Llumina sets the price. A 150-page book will retail for $13.95.

Author Purchases
Authors receive 30%-60% off retail, depending on volume. An order of 200 books receives a 50% discount.

Author Rights and Contract
Author retains all book rights and can cancel the contract with a 30-day written notice.

Strength
- They offer excellent distribution and some other nice features in the publishing package that make it a strong value.

Weaknesses
- Royalty payout is far lower than what other similarly priced firms offer.

Conclusion

Though the publishing package itself is a good value and the sales results have improved year after year, low royalty payments make this firm difficult to recommend.

Lulu Press, Inc.

SNAPSHOT

Overall Rating: Average

Royalties: Average

Sales Results: ★ ★ ★ ★ ★

Distribution: ★ ★ ★ ★ ★

Contact Info

www.lulu.com

Best Publishing Package

The total cost for publishing and distribution is $519. That price includes the Primer Pack for $369 and Global Distribution for $150. You get custom cover design, ebook option, one personal copy of your book, and advanced interior layout formatting. Lulu gives you the option to use your own ISBN if you choose. Package includes:

- ISBN
- Bar Code
- Books in Print
- Wholesalers – Ingram and Baker & Taylor
- Website Listings - Amazon.com, Barnes&Noble.com, and others

Services Available
Editing, marketing, formatting, scanning, and international distribution.

Trade Discounts
Lulu sets a 50% trade discount, which is enough for many bookstores to stock your book.

Retail Royalties
A $14.95 book of 150 pages sold on Amazon, or through any bookstore, will pay around $2.38 in royalties. See calculator at **lugaru.com/lulucalc.html**

Royalties through Publisher Website
A 150-page book for $14.95 will pay approximately $5.95 through Lulu.com.

Book Pricing
You control the pricing.

Author Purchases: Authors pay 50% of the retail price.

Author Rights and Contract
Authors retain full book rights and Lulu makes it easy to cancel the contract.

Strengths
- Lulu offers deep discounts that encourage retailers to stock your book on shelves without it coming at the expense of your royalty payments.
- Excellent distribution.
- Lulu was one of the first self-publishing firms in the industry and has a great deal of experience.

- This year saw a tremendous improvement in sales results over last year.

Weaknesses
- Lulu will only accept contact through email, and the website leaves many important questions unanswered, including pricing, royalties, and trade discounts. I had to submit a manuscript before Lulu would explain their publishing costs and services.

Conclusion
Lulu has long been a reputable company among writers. They pay fair royalties, offer excellent distribution, and have a record of strong book sales. To stand out (the way they once did) in this competitive market, however, they will have to offer more transparent information on the website and better customer service.

Mill City Press, Inc.

SNAPSHOT
Overall Value: Average   Royalties: Excellent

Sales Results: ★ ★ ★   Distribution: ★ ★ ★ ★ ★

Contact Info
Mill City Press   www.MillCityPress.net
212 3rd Ave N, # 290   email through website
Minneapolis, MN 55401   1-888-645-5248

Best Publishing Package

Mill City charges $1497 for a package with custom cover design, interior formatting, copyright registration, a five-page website for your book, submission to Google Books, Search Inside with Amazon, a marketing strategy session, and ten copies of your book. $25 annual listing fee. Package also includes:

- ISBN
- Bar Code
- Books in Print
- LCCN
- Wholesalers - Ingram and Baker & Taylor
- Website Listings - Amazon.com, Barnes&Noble.com, Borders.com, Powells.com, BooksaMillion.com, Alibris.com, Abebooks.com, and more

Services Available

Bookstore returns, marketing, website order fulfillment, editing, and ebook creation are available.

Trade Discounts

Mill City allows authors to set any discount up to 55%.

Timeline: Three to six weeks.

Retail Royalties

One-hundred percent of the retail price minus production cost and discounts. A $14.95 book sold with a 40% discount will pay $5.82 in royalties through Amazon or brick-and-mortar stores. Even at a 55% discount, royalties would be $2.72.

Book Pricing: You control the pricing.

Author Purchases
The cost of production, which is $3.15 for a 150-page book.

Author Rights and Contract
Author retains all rights to the book and materials. Mill City makes it easy to terminate the contract with written notice. They return all materials (cover art, text files) upon request.

Strengths
- Very high royalties—among the highest in the industry even when extending a 55% discount to retailers.
- Excellent author purchase prices for books.
- Excellent distribution.
- Very quick turnaround time.

Weakness
- Though this firm offers very professional services, the cost of publishing is high, and better deals may be found out there among the competition.

Conclusion
This publisher is fairly new to the market, but because they have shown they can produce successful titles and provide a very favorable offering to writers, Mill City has earned a spot among the profiled publishers. Their publishing package is among the most expensive of those I would consider recommending, but the high royalties, deep discounts, fast turnaround time, and low author purchase prices help offset the expensive upfront cost.

Morgan James

SNAPSHOT

Overall Rating: Not Recommended

Royalties: Poor to Average

Sales Results: ★ ★ ★ ★ ★

Distribution: ★ ★ ★ ★ ★

Contact Info

Morgan James Publishing
1225 Franklin Ave, # 325
Garden City, NY 11530

Morgan-James-Publishing.com
Email through website
1-800-485-4943

Best Publishing Package

Instead of publishing packages, Morgan James charges a membership fee of $4,995. The fee includes custom cover design, submission to Google Print, interior layout, ten copies of your book, advanced Ingram catalog, and online marketing classes. Also included are the creation and distribution of two media releases and a list of media contacts. Package includes:

- ISBN
- Bar Code
- Books in Print
- LCCN Wholesalers – Ingram and Baker & Taylor
- Website Listings - Amazon.com, Barnes&Noble.com, Borders.com, and more

Trade Discounts: They set the discount at 45-55%.

Timeline: Three months.

Retail Royalties

Twenty percent, though they will not clarify what the twenty percent is based on. Morgan James does not provide information on their production costs. A rough estimate shows them paying somewhere between $1.00 and $3.00 in royalties for a 150-page $14.95 book.

Book Pricing: They control the pricing. A 150-page book will sell for around $14.95.

Author Purchases
Authors pay production cost.

Strength
- High rate of success with book sales.

Weaknesses
- $4995 is very expensive for book publishing.
- They are not straightforward about their business model and lack transparency.
- Royalty payments are unclear and are likely lower than the industry average.

Conclusion
Morgan James prefers to position itself outside the scope of self-publishing and has convinced a number authors that they are a traditional publisher because they don't charge for a publishing package. They charge a pricey membership fee instead.

Though Morgan James has fantastic sales results, the sales still aren't enough to offset the high cost of publishing and poor royalty payments. These shortcomings, combined with their shady business tactics, have earned them a below average rating overall.

Outskirts Press

SNAPSHOT

Overall Rating: Excellent

Sales Results: ★★★★

Royalties: Average

Distribution: ★★★★★

Contact Info

Outskirts Press, Inc.
10940 S. Parker Rd. Suite 515
Parker, CO 80134

www.OutskirtsPress.com
Info@OutskirtsPress.com
1-888-OP-BOOKS

Best Publishing Package

The Sapphire Package for $399 is the best value and includes a webpage on the publisher's site, a choice of six customizable covers, and one copy of your book. Annual listing fee is $25.00. Package includes:

- ISBN
- Bar Code
- Books in Print
- Wholesalers - Ingram
- Website Listings - Amazon.com, Barnes&Noble.com, Powells.com, Amazon.co.uk, and BooksaMillion.com

Full Color: Outskirts also offers a Pearl Package for $1099 for color interiors. This package offers all the perks of the Ruby Package, but gives you full color printing on cover as well as the inside pages. See the website for more details.

Services Available

Custom cover design, editing, ebook formatting, indexing, marketing, promotional materials, submission to book fairs, and press releases.

Trade Discounts
Authors can set discounts up to 55%.

Timeline: Ten to thirteen weeks.

Retail Royalties
A 150-page book that retails for $14.95 will pay $2.64. This assumes a 40% discount. Authors can set it higher or lower and the royalties will be affected accordingly. The Pearl Package (full color) pays $2.00 for a 150 page color book that would retail for $42.95. Outskirts has a useful royalties calculator found at **www.outskirtspress.com/calculator.php.**

Royalties from Publisher Website
Same as Retail Royalties. See above.

Book Pricing: You control the pricing.

Author Purchases
A 150-page book that retails for $14.95 will cost $6.43 a copy.

Author Rights and Contract
Authors retain full book rights and Outskirts makes it easy to terminate the contract.

Strengths
- Outskirts offers a rare and exceptional value for $399 that includes excellent distribution.
- The flexibility in setting book price and discounts, including the option to offer a 55% discount for bookshelf stocking.
- Though the royalties are average, Outskirts offers you the flexibility of lowering the discount to 20% to increase them.

Conclusion

Outskirts does everything well and they have years of experience behind them. With incredibly competitive pricing for publishing packages and excellent sales results, Outskirts earns another year of an Excellent overall rating.

They have a reputation in the industry for treating authors fairly and running a solid business.

Pleasant Word

SNAPSHOT

Overall Rating: Not Recommended

Royalties: Poor

Sales Results: ★ ★

Distribution: ★ ★ ★ ★ ★

Pleasant Word is a Christian firm and a division of the traditional publisher, WinePress Publishing.

Contact Info

Pleasant Word

1730 Railroad St.

Enumclaw, WA 98022

www.PleasantWord.com

Email through website

1-800-326-4674

Best Publishing Package

The Yellow Ribbon Package for $1299 includes bookstore returns, custom cover design, formatting, bookstore returns, and ten copies of your book. Also included:

- ISBN
- Bar Code

- LCCN
- Wholesalers – Ingram and Baker & Taylor
- Website Listings - Amazon.com, Barnes&Noble.com

Services Available
Marketing, publicity, and editing.

Trade Discounts
Discounts are 50 to 57%.

Timeline: Three to four months.

Retail Royalties
One-hundred percent of the retail price minus production cost and discounts. According to their website, a 200 pg page book retailing for $17.99 book will pay $1.26 for Amazon and $3.95 for brick-and-mortar sales. To see sample calculations, go to **www.pleasantword.com/guides/royalties.asp**

Royalties through Publisher Website
One-hundred percent of the retail price minus production cost and $1.95 for handling.

Book Pricing: Pleasant Word sets the price. A 150-page book will retail for $15.99.

Author Purchases
Authors receive 58% off the retail price.

Author Rights and Contract
Author retains book rights and can cancel the contract at any time.

Strengths

- Excellent distribution.
- A 55% discount increases the odds that your book will be presented on bookstore shelves.

Weakness

- Amazon royalties are among the lowest in the industry.
- Book sales are not as strong as other firms.

Conclusion

Though bookstore royalties are higher than average, the firm does not earn better marks because the sales are a bit weak and the Amazon royalties are too low.

Tate Publishing

SNAPSHOT

Overall Rating: Not Recommended   **Royalties:** Average

Sales Results: ★ ★ ★   **Distribution:** ★ ★ ★ ★

Contact Info

Tate Publishing
127 East Trade Center Terrace
Mustang, OK 73064

www.TatePublishing.com
Email through website
1-405-376-4900

Best Publishing Package

Tate charges $3895 to publish a book. The package includes hands-on editorial services, custom cover design, audio book formatting, bookstore returns, and ebook formatting. Package also includes:

- ISBN
- Bar Code
- Books in Print
- LCCN - Included
- Wholesalers – Ingram
- Website Listings - Amazon.com and Barnes&Noble.com

Trade Discounts: Unclear

Timeline: Unclear

Retail Royalties

From the limited information we were able to obtain from Tate, the royalty appears to be fifteen percent of the retail price—$2.24 for a $14.95 book.

Royalties through Publisher Website

Forty percent of retail price, so a $14.95 book will pay $5.98 on sales through Tate's website.

Author Purchases

Authors receive 60% off the retail price, which is $5.98 for a $14.95 book.

Author Rights and Contract

Author retains all book rights.

Strength

- The publishing package includes a lot of strong perks, including editorial service, bookstore returns, and audio and ebook formatting.

Weaknesses

- Tate has a history of making claims that it's a traditional publisher but fails to offer any of the benefits of traditional publishing.
- Sales are not as strong as we've seen in other firms.
- It is unclear what trade discount Tate offers.

Conclusion

Publishing costs are high, royalties are low, and practices are shady. Among other shortcomings, Tate is the only publisher in this directory that matches very high publishing prices with very low sales performances.

Trafford Publishing

SNAPSHOT

Overall Rating: Average	Royalties: Below Average
Sales Results: ★ ★ ★ ★	Distribution: ★ ★ ★ ★ ★

Trafford is one of several self-publishing companies owned by parent company Author Solutions. Trafford is independently operated and maintains its own policies.

Contact Info

Trafford Publishing
1663 Liberty Dr.
Bloomington IN 47403

www.Trafford.com
Info@Trafford.com
1-888-232-4444

Best Publishing Package

The Prime package for $799 includes custom cover design, one round of proof corrections, book design and interior page layout, and a personal web page on the Trafford website. Full color interior publishing is available, starting at $999. The packages also include:

- ISBN
- Bar Code
- Books in Print
- Wholesalers - Ingram and Baker & Taylor
- Website Listings - Amazon.com, Barnes&Noble.com, Borders.com

Services Available

Bookseller returns, editing, marketing, and promotion.

Trade Discounts

A 36% discount accompanies a 20% royalty. Authors have the option to extend a 50% discount to retailers in exchange for a 10% royalty payment.

Retail Royalties

Ten to 20% of the list price (depending on your discount) after discounts, taxes, and shipping are subtracted. A book priced at $14.95 will pay $1.91 using the 36% discount and 20% royalty. Using the 50% discount and 10% royalty, payment would be $0.75.

Royalties through Publisher Website

A 150-page book selling for $14.95 will pay around $2.99 through the Trafford website.

Book Pricing

Trafford sets the minimum price. A 150-page book starts at $14.70 and you can raise the price to increase your royalties.

Author Purchases

A 150-page book will cost you $7.00 for one copy. An order for 250 copies will cost $6.37 per book.

Author Rights and Contract

Authors retain full book rights. Contract can be cancelled with 30 days written notice.

Strengths

- Excellent distribution.
- The option to offer aggressive discounts and encourage bookstores to stock your book.
- $799 is a solid value because it includes cover design and a round of free proof correction. Most firms charge for any changes to the proof.
- Sales have improved over last year.

Weaknesses

- Royalties are below the industry average.
- Trafford is not as forthcoming about hard numbers as other firms covered in this book.

Conclusion

Trafford has improved its ratings from the first edition. They have begun to consistently offer reasonable prices, an easy to use (though still incomplete) website, and have continued to demonstrate growing book sales. I like what they offer in the publishing package but need to see higher royalties before I can give them a stronger recommendation.

Universal Publishers

SNAPSHOT

Overall Rating: Average

Royalties: Average

Sales Results: ★ ★

Distribution: ★ ★ ★ ★ ★

Contact Info

Universal Publishers, Inc.
23331 Water Circle
Boca Raton, FL 33486

www.Universal-Publishers.com
Email through website
No phone number

Best Publishing Package

The $495 package includes a generic cover and a web page on the publisher's site. Custom cover is $100 additional. Universal will knock $100 off the package price if you can convert your document to a PDF on your own. Package includes:

- ISBN
- Bar Code
- Books in Print
- Wholesalers – Ingram and Baker & Taylor
- Website Listings - Amazon.com, Barnes&Noble.com

Services Available

Custom cover design for $100.

Trade Discounts

Universal offers a 40% discount to retailers, which means your book will be available for special order upon request, but it will not be presented on bookstore shelves.

Timeline: Two to three months.

Retail Royalties
Universal pays 10% of the retail price, (down from 20% a year ago) regardless of production cost and discounts. A $25.95 book (the lowest price allowable by Universal) will earn $2.59 in royalties.

Universal has a policy of paying royalties only after the first three copies have been sold each quarter. This means they keep the profit on the first three copies instead of paying you. At three a quarter, that's twelve books a year you don't get paid for.

Royalties through Publisher Website
Twenty percent of the retail price.

Book Pricing
Universal sets the price. Books up to 300 pages retail for $25.95.

Author Purchases
Authors receive 40%-50% off the retail price. A 150-page book will retail for $25.95 and cost the author $15.57 a copy.

Author Rights and Contract
Author retains book rights and can cancel the contract with a 90-day written notice.

Strengths
- $495 is a great value for what Universal offers and the additional $100 for a custom cover is a good package.

Weaknesses

- Their pricing of $25.95 for a 150-page book is too high. A bit of research quickly reveals that paperback books simply do not sell at that price, which helps explain their overall anemic book sales.
- Because of the high book pricing, author purchased books are the most expensive in the industry.
- They don't pay royalties on the first three sales of every quarter.

Conclusion

Reduced royalties from two years ago remain a huge disappointment. The mediocre sales and high book pricing prevent Universal from receiving a strong recommendation.

Virtual Bookworm Publishing

SNAPSHOT

Overall Rating: Excellent

Sales Results: ★ ★ ★ ★

Royalties: Above Average

Distribution: ★ ★ ★ ★ ★

Contact Info

VirtualBookworm
P.O. Box 9949
College Station, TX 77842

www.VirtualBookworm.com
Email through website
1-877-376-4955

Best Publishing Package

The Level A Soft Cover Package for $360 is one of the best values in the industry. It includes cover design with author photo and bio on back, one free copy of the book, copyright application kit, up to fifteen images, and a page on their website. Ebook formatting is also available. Color publishing is available starting at $625. Packages include:

- ISBN
- Bar Code
- Books in Print
- Wholesalers - Ingram and Baker & Taylor
- Website Listings - Amazon.com, Borders.com

Services Available
Marketing packages, ebook formatting starting at $65, editing, and internal warehousing.

Trade Discounts
You can set average or aggressive discounts.

Retail Royalties
Fifty percent of the retail price minus production cost and discounts. A 120-page book sold on Amazon or at any retailer (with a 30% discount) for $12.95 will pay $3.18.

Royalties through Publisher Website
Thirty percent of the retail price.

Book Pricing
They set the price—$12.95 for 150-page book.

Author Purchases
Authors receive 30%-50% off the cover price.

Author Rights and Contract
Author retains all book rights. Virtual Bookworm charges a $50 contract termination fee.

Strengths
- You will be hard pressed to find a better publishing price that includes as many benefits as this one.
- Excellent sales results.
- Improved website over previous years.
- Excellent distribution.
- Flexibility in setting trade discounts.
- Above average royalties.

Conclusion
An exceptional self-publishing firm, Virtual Bookworm proves that you don't have to spend thousands to succeed in self-publishing. They deliver outstanding products and services for an incredible price. With stellar sales results and a great value for the money, you can't go wrong here. Virtual Bookworm is among the favorites.

Wheatmark

SNAPSHOT

Overall Rating: Average

Sales Results: ★ ★ ★ ★

Royalties: Poor

Distribution: ★ ★ ★ ★ ★

Contact Info

Wheatmark, Inc.
610 East Delano St. #104
Tucson, AZ 85705

www.Wheatmark.com
Info@Wheatmark.com
1-888-934-0888

Best Publishing Package

The Basic Package for $1299 includes bookstore returns, cover design, and five copies of your book. Full color interior options are available. Packages include:

- ISBN
- Bar Code
- Books in Print
- LCCN
- Wholesalers - Ingram and Baker & Taylor
- Website Listings - Amazon.com, Barnes&Noble.com, Borders.com, Borders.com, BooksaMillion.com, Target.com

Services Available

Marketing, editing, custom cover design, indexing, footnoting, and interior layout support.

Trade Discounts: Wheatmark discounts 55%, which means bookstores will be more likely to stock your book on the shelves.

Timeline: Four months.

Retail Royalties
Twenty percent of what the third party retailer pays Wheatmark for your book. Or put another way, 20% of the retail price after the discount is deducted, regardless of the production cost. A $14.95 book will pay $1.35 in royalties.

Royalties through Publisher Website
Twenty percent of the retail price minus the production cost.

Book Pricing
Wheatmark sets a reasonable minimum price ($13.95 for a 150-page book) and you can raise it from there.

Author Purchases
Authors receive 40-75% off the retail price, depending on volume. An order of 250 books is discounted 50%.

Author Rights and Contract
Authors retain full book rights. Wheatmark allows easy contract cancellation with a thirty day written notice.

Strengths
- Excellent distribution.
- Excellent track record of strong sales.
- Deep discounts to retailers.
- The publishing package includes cover design and bookstore returns.

Weaknesses
- Royalties are below the industry average. That is only partially due to the 55% discount given to retailers.

- Wheatmark makes finding information about their offerings difficult. Greater transparency would boost ratings.

Conclusion

Wheatmark has improved its sales sharply since the last publication, giving them greater appeal. The publishing package, though expensive, is a good value. If you are serious about brick and mortar sales, the 55% discount combined with the bookstore returns make this a good choice. I'd like to give Wheatmark a higher rating, but the low royalties and lack of openness and information prevent it.

WingSpan Press

SNAPSHOT

Overall Rating: Good	Royalties: Above Average
Sales Results: ★ ★	Distribution: ★ ★ ★ ★

Contact Info

WingSpan Press
P.O. Box 2085
Livermore, CA 94551

www.WingSpanPress.com
Info@WingSpanPress.com
1-866-735-3782

Best Publishing Package

WingSpan's Standard Package for $499 includes interior layout, basic cover design, back cover creation, printing on 20% post-consumer acid free paper, and one copy of your book. Package also includes:

- ISBN
- Bar Code
- Books in Print
- LCCN
- Wholesalers - Ingram
- Website Listings - Amazon.com, Barnes&Noble.com, Borders.com, and more

Services Available
Custom cover design, layout, copyright registration, footnoting, editing, and marketing.

Trade Discounts
Unclear. The website and contract say nothing about discounts. When I contacted them they wouldn't discuss trade discounts, explaining that "bookstores are a poor place to sell books."

Timeline: Six to eight weeks

Retail Royalties
Twenty percent of the retail price, regardless of production cost or discounts. A 150-page book selling for $14.95 will pay $2.99 for sales on Amazon or through any bookstore.

Royalties through Publisher Website
Buyers are redirected to Amazon.com.

Book Pricing
WingSpan sets a price that you can adjust up or down by $2.00. They price a 150-page book at $12.95.

Author Purchases
Authors pay production cost plus shipping. Production cost for a 150-page book runs about $4.15. Offset printing is available for orders of 1000+ books, which further reduces the cost.

Author Rights and Contract
Author retains all book rights. WingSpan makes it easy to cancel the contract.

Strengths
- WingSpan offers an excellent value at $499.
- Strong sales results.
- One of the better author purchase prices in the industry.
- Offset printing availability for large orders.
- Quick turnaround time.

Weakness
- WingSpan has demonstrated strong sales results in the past but appears to be slipping in the rankings over last year's results.

Conclusion
WingSpan is small self-publishing firm that delivers a lot for a great price. Their affordable package, above average royalties, quick timeline, and low price for author purchases make them a worthwhile option.

Xlibris Corporation

SNAPSHOT

Overall Rating: Average

Royalties: Poor

Sales Results: ★ ★ ★ ★

Distribution: ★ ★ ★ ★ ★

Xlibris is owned by parent company Author Solutions but is independently operated and maintains its own policies.

Contact Info

Xlibris Corporation
1663 Liberty Drive #200
Bloomington IN 47403

www2.Xlibris.com
info@Xlibris.com
1-888-795-4274

Best Publishing Package

The Advantage Package for $449 includes one copy of your book, choice of three cover templates, and choice of two interior templates. Full color interior publishing is also available for $499. Package also includes:

- ISBN
- Bar Code
- Books in Print
- Wholesalers – Ingram and Baker & Taylor
- Website Listings - Amazon.com, Barnes&Noble.com, Borders.com, and many more

Services Available

Marketing, editing, leather bound editions, indexing, citation service, copyright registration, bookstore returns, and much more.

Trade Discounts

Xlibris offers a 40% discount, which will prevent bookstores from stocking your book but still allow orders upon request.

Retail Royalties

Ten percent of the retail price when you let them set the price ($1.99 for a $19.99 book) If you set your own price, your royalties for a 150 page book priced at $15.99 (lowest price allowable by Xlibris) will pay $1.00 in royalties on books sold through any outlet.

Royalties through Publisher Website

Twenty-five percent of the retail price.

Book Pricing

Xlibris sets the price—$19.99 for a 150-page book. For a fee of $249, Xlibris will let you set your own book price, however, the lowest allowable price for a 150-page book is $15.99.

Author Purchases

Authors receive 30-60% off the retail price, depending on volume.

Author Rights and Contract

Author retains all book rights. Xlibris makes it easy to cancel the contract.

Strengths

- The $449 publishing package is a very good value that includes cover as well as interior templates and excellent distribution.
- Xlibris has a solid record of strong book sales.
- They offer a large selection of add-on services.

Weaknesses

- The price they set for a 150-page book ($19.99) is too high.
- With the high retail price they assign to books, Xlibris has no excuse for paying such low royalties.
- Author purchased books are expensive.

Conclusion

A generous publishing package and strong distribution combined with low royalty payments and an inflated minimum book price earned Xlibris a mediocre rating here. Unless you are a famous author, you will have trouble selling a book for $19.99 when New York Times Best Sellers are going for considerably less.

Xulon Press

SNAPSHOT

Overall Rating: Excellent

Royalties: Above Average

Sales Results: ★ ★ ★ ★

Distribution: ★ ★ ★ ★ ★

Xulon Press publishes books that support Christian values. If Xulon does not feel a book upholds their values they will not publish it.

Contact Info

Xulon Press
2180 West State Rd. 434, # 2140
Longwood, FL 32779

www.XulonPress.com
1-866-381-2665

Best Publishing Package
The Premium Package for $1199 offers cover design, interior formatting, insertion of page numbers and headers, two copies of your book, and distribution to Christian bookstores. $25 annual listing fee. Full color packages with distribution start at $1699 start at Included are:

- ISBN
- Bar Code
- Books in Print
- Wholesalers – Ingram and Christian Book Distributors
- Website Listings - Amazon.com, Barnes&Noble.com, Borders.com, Target.com, Christianbook.com

Services Available
Editing, international distribution, bookstore returns, and copyright filing are also available.

Trade Discounts: You can set a 40%-60% discount.
Timeline: Up to three months.

Retail Royalties
One-hundred percent of the retail price minus production cost and discounts. Xulon is not forthcoming on what they charge for production, claiming that the prices are different for every book and fluctuate throughout the year. However, this fluctuation doesn't happen with other publishers. An estimate provided by Xulon shows a $15.99 book sold on Amazon or at any bookstore with a 55% discount paying around $3.30.

Xulon pays royalties only twice a year. Once in August and again in February.

Royalties through Publisher Website
Seventy-five percent of the retail price minus production cost.

Book Pricing
Xulon sets the price based on the number of pages ($14.99 for a 150-page book).

Author Purchases
Thirty-five to 70% off the retail price based on volume. An order of 200 books will be discounted 50%.

Author Rights and Contract
Author retains all book rights and Xulon makes it easy to cancel the contract.

Strengths
- Flexibility to offer deep discounts to retailers.
- Xulon maintains a high royalty payment in conjunction with deep discounts to retailers. Big plus.
- Distribution is excellent for the Christian book market.
- Sales performance has increased over last year.

Weaknesses
- $1199 for publishing is on the high end for what you get in return.
- Royalty payments only twice a year make Xulon a tough choice for those looking for a career in writing.

Conclusion
If your book stands to benefit from the Christian Bookstore distribution offered at Xulon, this firm may, in fact, be the best choice you can make for your book.

	Sales Results	Amazon Royalty	Bookstore Royalty
AuthorHouse	★★★★	$2.24	$2.24
Aventine Press	★★★★	$2.68	$2.68
BookLocker	★★★★	$2.24	$2.24
BookPros	★★★★★	$6.15	$6.15
CreateSpace	★★★★★	$6.32	$3.33
Creation House	★★★★	$0.75	$0.75
Dog Ear	★★★★★	$4.69	$4.69
Foremost Press	★★★	$2.39	$2.39
Infinity Publishing	★★★★	$2.24	$2.24
iUniverse	★★★★★	$1.91	$1.91
Llumina Press	★★★	$1.40	$1.40
Lulu Press, Inc.	★★★★★	$2.38	$2.38
Mill City Press	★★★	$5.82	$5.82
Morgan James	★★★★★	$2.00	$2.00
Outskirts Press	★★★★	$2.64	$2.64
Pleasant Word	★★	$1.26*	$3.95*
Tate Publishing	★★★	$2.24	$2.24
Trafford Publishing	★★★★	$1.91	$1.91
Universal Publishers	★★	$2.59 **	$2.59 **
VirtualBookworm	★★★★	$3.18	$3.18
Wheatmark	★★★★	$1.35	$1.35
WingSpan Press	★★	$2.99	$2.99
Xlibris	★★★★	$1.99	$1.99
Xulon Press	★★★★	$3.30	$3.30

All numbers based on a 150-page, $14.95 book. *$17.99 retail price.

TOP SELF PUBLISHING FIRMS

Best Package	Distribution	Author Purchases	Overall Rating	Page
$599	★★★★★	$7.00	Good	52
$399	★★★★	$3.47	Excellent	54
$299	★★★★	$9.72	Good	56
$17,800	★★★★★	$4.40	Not Rec.	59
$39	★★★	$2.65	Excellent	63
$22,400	★★★★	$11.20	Not Rec.	66
$1,099	★★★★★	$4.28	Excellent	68
$347	★★★★★	$7.48	Good	71
$499	★★★★★	$6.72	Good	73
$599	★★★★★	$8.97	Average	75
$799	★★★★★	$8.97	Not Rec.	79
$519	★★★★★	$7.47	Average	81
$1,497	★★★★★	$3.15	Average	83
$4,995	★★★★★	X	Not Rec.	86
$399	★★★★★	$6.43	Excellent	88
$1299	★★★★★	$6.72	Not Rec.	90
$3,895	★★★★	$5.98	Not Rec.	92
$799	★★★★★	$6.37	Average	94
$495	★★★★★	$15.57	Average	97
$360	★★★★★	$8.97	Excellent	99
$1299	★★★★★	$7.48	Average	102
$499	★★★★	$4.15	Good	104
$499	★★★★★	$9.00	Average	107
$1,199	★★★★★	$7.47	Excellent	109

** $25.95 retail price.

7
Best Selling Genres for Self-Published Books

Your genre will determine your reading audience, which will ultimately determine your book's potential for sales. Self-published authors find success in many of the same categories as do conventional publishers. If one of your goals in writing is to succeed financially, consider the role that subject matter will play in the demand for your book. Often a book succeeds in spite of its mediocre writing because there is such strong interest in the topic.

The best way to stack the odds for success in your favor is to find a successful genre you like and then write a niche book within that category. For example, instead of a general how-to book on landscaping, write about landscaping for water conservation with drought tolerant plants or planting a yard with native species for different geographic areas. By focusing on a more specific topic, you will set your book apart from the competition and create a product of real value to a targeted audience of people who can use it.

Alternatively, you can write about a general topic but target a specific audience. For example, you could write about landscaping but target allergy sufferers, those on a tight budget, or city dwellers seeking green space. By narrowing your audience you will actually increase your sales. If you need convincing, look back through the list of successful titles in chapters two and three and observe how many general topic books you see there verses the number of very specific subjects. A niche book will be easier to market and much more likely to see strong sales.

Though there are exceptions, nearly 90% of all successful self-published books fall into the categories described here.

#1 How-To

Largely because of the success of online booksellers, How-To has become, by far, the top selling category for self-published books. Need information on taming feral kittens? Type the key words into Amazon. Want to learn more about the top dental hygiene schools? Search Barnes&Noble.com and you'll find the book you need.

If you want to write how-to books, you must either be an authority in the subject or become one through interviews and research. Being an expert doesn't necessarily require an advanced degree or years of experience. For example, Mike Doolin wrote *A Guerrilla Manual for Adult College Students* to help others succeed where he had struggled as an adult returning to college. Direct mail to community college bookstores, along with an informative website, generated a flood of requests for his book. College bookstores placed volume orders and invited Doolin to speak at campuses around the country.

A well written and researched how-to book can sell for years if the material does not become obsolete. The best how-to books are organized, have titles specific to the topic, and don't assume too much or too little about what the reader already knows.

Current top selling, self-published how-to titles include:

- *Writing for Emotional Impact,* by Karl Iglesias
- *How to REALLY use LinkedIn,* by Jan Vermeiren
- *Everything the Instructors Never Told You About Mogul Skiing,* by Dan DiPiro

#2 Fiction

Although fiction comes in second on the list of bestselling genres, don't make the mistake of thinking it's easy to succeed. The market is flooded with thousands of fiction books that are not selling. If you want to shine, be prepared to work hard. Your book, as well as your marketing efforts, must be outstanding.

Within fiction writing, the top selling self-published books belong almost exclusively to four genres:

- Historical Fiction
- Mystery / Thriller
- Romance
- Science Fiction

Several self-published authors have shown that successful fiction writing is possible. They have demonstrated that great results are repeatable by publishing multiple books that outperform the market. Lynn Galli has four novels performing in the top 15%: *Uncommon Emotions, Wasted Heart, Imagining Reality,* and her most recent *Blessed Twice.* In another example, Rhiannon Frater has a very successful zombie trilogy, *As the World Dies.* All three books are currently selling at a very impressive top 3% of the market.

#3 Health and Fitness

Every year these books rise to the top of the bestseller list. Despite the hundreds of related titles already on the market, readers crave more. This genre is not just limited to weight loss books. Links between nutrition and the brain have parents making homemade baby food and baby boomers drinking pomegranate juice. Thanks to Google and LexisNexis, you don't have to be a nutritionist to write a book on the benefits of vitamin supplements or the risks of diabetes; you just have to know how to research.

New Year's resolutions usually have a weight loss or fitness element, so if your book teaches people to lose weight, launch a well-timed marketing campaign to take advantage of the sales spike that happens right after the first of the year.

Current self-published top sellers include:
- *Your Healing Diet: A Quick Guide to Reversing Psoriasis and Chronic Diseases with Healing Foods,* by Deirdre Earls
- *Raising a Vaccine Free Child,* by Wendy Lydall
- *Laparoscopic Adjustable Gastric Banding,* by Jessie H. Ahroni

#4 Self-Help / Self-Improvement

From surviving divorce to improving your appearance, self-help titles occupy a lot of real estate on bookstore shelves. If you have something to teach about self-defense, parenting a disabled child, or dealing with addiction, write a book to help others benefit from your knowledge.

Personal experience and understanding of an issue, paired with great writing, can lead to big book sales. After fifty publishers rejected his book, Terrence Shulman smartened up and published, *Something for Nothing: Shoplifting Addiction and Recovery,* with Infinity. Since the launch of his book, Shulman has appeared on Oprah, CNN, Fox News, and the Discovery Channel. Thanks to the success of his book, Shulman is considered an expert in his field.

Current self-published Self Help books include:
- *The Enabler: When Helping Hurts the Ones You Love,* by Angelyn Miller
- *The Life of Your Dreams in 30 Days or Less!* by Cindy Day
- *The Zen of Meeting Women,* by Max Weiss

#5 Religion

Religious books are one of the top selling categories for self-publishers. You don't have to be a biblical scholar or a rabbi to excel in this category. Books about applying religion in everyday life are just as popular as scholarly writing.

Inspiration can come from surprising places. It was concern over the accuracy of translations in the Hebrew Bible that led Jeff Benner to publish nine books with Virtual Bookworm. Among them are *A Mechanical Translation of the Books of Genesis* and *The Ancient Hebrew Language and Alphabet.* All nine of his books remain in the top 20% of Amazon sales.

#6 Business

Business makes the world go round and if you have something valuable to contribute you will have a lot of competition but also plenty of readers. If you're writing in business, write on what you know. If you have management, leadership, or executive experience, you are qualified to write a business book. If you've worked in marketing, customer service, or accounting, you have information others need.

The top selling self-published business books cover the usual topics: motivation, consulting, making money with stocks, and secrets to success. More specific topics include the Fair Tax, tips on acquiring Social Security, and making money with MySpace.

Top selling self-published titles in Business include:
- *The Sixty-Second Motivator,* by Jim Johnson
- *The Maui CEO: Import from China, Sell on eBay, and Live Wherever You Want,* by John Tennant
- *SEO Made Simple: Strategies For Dominating The World's Largest Search Engine,* by Michael H. Fleischner

#7 Personal Story

Being famous, being related to a famous person, or having close contact with fame will serve you well in this genre. A book about your experience as Michael Jordan's personal trainer is bound to sell volumes. However, if you have no such celebrity in your life, you are not entirely out of luck.

Outside of prominent name titles, smart authors have found a way to carve out a personal story by writing niche books. Without fame, no one will read the story of your life. On the other hand, someone *might* read the story of living with a life threatening disease. In *Learning to Be Me: My Twenty-Three Year Battle with Bulimia,* author Jocelyn Golden strikes a chord with readers. Her story is compelling because it is not the story of her life but rather a depiction of how one thing influenced her life story. If you want your personal story to sell in the top 8% for thirty-eight consecutive weeks, as this one has, it must focus on a subject that will interest people.

Some top selling examples include:
- *My Husband's Affair Became the Best Thing That Ever Happened to Me,* by Anne Bercht
- *Out in Bad Standings: Inside the Bandidos Motorcycle Club,* by Edward Winterhalder
- *Realities of Foreign Service Life,* by Patricia Linderman

#8 Travel

Would you like to make money while vacationing? You can sell books about your travel experiences and take a tax deduction at the same time. If you travel often to the same place and know all of the best restaurants and hotels in the area, share it with the rest of us. If high-end, movie-star destinations fascinate you, go check them out for yourself and publish your findings.

Your best chance for success with travel writing is with a niche subject in a well-known area or a lesser-known destination that has yet to be thoroughly covered. You can create new areas of interest by writing about up-and-coming locations or specific slivers in existing hot spots. For example, you could compile a directory of the best boutiques on the west coast or write the definitive book on doing business in Vietnam. You want a subject that doesn't have too much established competition but has enough interest to sell books. A book about Europe is fine if you can find a way to approach Europe differently than the hundreds of other European travel books on the market.

Travel writing is a great way to see the world and can open the door to additional travel opportunities. Take John La Plante for instance, who wrote, *Around the World at 75, Alone, Dammit!* The book covered practical tips and information for traveling alone in twenty countries.

La Plante described his book to a fellow traveler who decided to buy the rights to the book for sale in China. La Plante was invited to Shanghai for the launch where his book sold by the thousands. When you write about travel, you never know where your readers will turn up.

Take at look at these top selling titles:

- *Mexico City: An Opinionated Guide for the Curious Traveler,* by Jim Johnston

- *Rome with Kids: An Insider's Guide,* by J.M. Pasquesi
- *Living and Retiring in Hawaii: The 50th State in the 21st Century,* by James R. Smith

#9 Professional Guides

Professional guides teach people how to land a job or improve performance in a current position. If you have a career, you can write a professional guide. The experience you have in your field is valuable to anyone interested in entering the profession or moving up from within. You can be successful by sharing basic information with a targeted audience of people who need it.

The experience of working hard and achieving success in a career is qualification to coach others to do the same. Again, you don't have to be an expert in your profession, but you do have to be accomplished enough to have information that others can use. The following top selling titles show how professionals share what they know.

- *The Pink Pocket Poser: The Glamour Photographers Posing Guide,* by Nigel Holmes
- *Becoming a Police Officer: An Insiders Guide,* by Barry Baker
- *From Zero to Hero: How to Master the Art of Selling Cars*, by Jeffrey Knott

Call upon your own experience and package it in a way that teaches. Even if you don't feel your profession is anything special, you will likely have information to offer people who are just starting out. Moreover, if you have become an expert in your field, by all means, teach the rest of us the secrets to your success.

#10 Personal Finance and Investing

Everyone at some point wishes for more money. Perhaps this is why so many titles, sold each year, teach people to earn more and spend less. The concepts are basic, but judging by the large number of top selling books in this category, there must be quite a bit more to it. Topics range from stock investing to paying down credit card debt.

Expertise in any field will serve your writing, but you don't have to be a CFO to write a top selling finance book. If you can create a family budget, cut household costs, or create a college savings system for your kids, you might already be on your way to the next bestseller.

Top sellers currently include:
- *A Trader on Wall Street: A Short Term Traders Guide,* by Michael Coval
- *Web of Debt: The Shocking Truth About Our Money System,* by Ellen Hodgson Brown
- *Profit from Prices: All You Need for Profit in Stock Trading is Stock Prices,* by Jayesh Patel

#11 Metaphysics and Paranormal

This category can include any topic beyond the range of normal experience or scientific explanation. Big Foot, UFO's, and out of body experiences fall into the metaphysical or paranormal. Teacher and career writer Karen Bishop has five books in this genre (published with BookLocker) currently selling in the top 20%. In another example, writer and historian Maximillien De Lafayette has twenty-one books on UFO's and alien life. Largely published by CreateSpace, at least half of his UFO titles are in the top 25% on Amazon at any given time.

Top sellers in Metaphysics and Paranormal include:
- *Grimorium Verum,* by Joseph H. Peterson
- *The Dead Walk Diaries,* by Joe Young
- *What Extraterrestrials and Anunnaki Want You to Know,* by Maximillien De Lafayette

#12 Food and Cooking

One way to write for this genre is to find a popular subject that interests you and put your own unique slant on it. You could write an entire book about preparing marinades or cooking for common food allergies. Food books need not be limited to recipe compilations. You can teach everything you know about a piece of kitchen equipment, or create a collection of cooking techniques from around the world. Whatever you choose, be specific in your topic.

Thanks to quick turnaround time, self-publishing is especially effective for cookbooks that are inspired by health trends, new kitchen devices, and diet fads. Traditional publishers turn down many of these books simply because they can't bring them to the market soon enough. Seize an opportunity and you may find you have no competition.

Check out these top sellers:
- *Meat Smoking and Smokehouse Design*, by Stanley Marianski
- *Freezer Bag Cooking: Trail Food Made Simple*, by Sarah Svien Kirkconnell
- *More Easy Beans: Quick and Tasty Bean, Pea and Lentil Recipes*, by Trish Ross

#13 Computers and Technology

The popularity of the internet and computers has spurred an entire new category of bestsellers. Constant advancements in technology offer plenty of fresh subject matter every year. Changes happen fast in this industry and with a self-publisher, you can respond more quickly than your traditionally published competitors can.

You don't have to be a computer science expert to write books in this genre, though it certainly helps. If you can use popular software, for instance, target others who want to improve their skills. Write books suited to your expertise, but aim for an audience that knows less than you do.

Don't assume that what comes easily to you even makes sense to other people. The internet and computers are so much a part of our everyday lives that we often take for granted what we know. You may find you don't have to look far to find a niche.

If you write in this genre, remember that your book will become obsolete as technology changes. You will need to accept that or find a way to produce multiple editions to stay up on the advancements. Top sellers in Computers and Technology include:

- *Servicing ITIL: A Handbook of IT Services for ITIL Managers and Practitioners*, by Randy A. Steinberg
- *BlackBerry Tour 9600 Made Simple,* by Martin Trautschold
- *Mastering Search Advertising: How the Top 3%. of Search Advertisers Dominate Google AdWords*, by Rich Stokes

#14 Animals

From breed directories to cute anecdotal stories, animal books see big sales every year. A niche book in this category can get a lot of mileage out of targeted promotion. A book on caring for a specific breed of dog, for example, may not appeal to most of the public, but if it's good it can sell to every owner of the breed, as did *The Havanese.*

Thirty years of experience breeding and showing purebred dogs led Diane Klumb to create a book for dog lovers, specifically Havanese dog owners. Aiming to produce the best book, Klumb collaborated with veterinarian Joanne Baldwin and eventually published with BookSurge. To get the word out, Klumb and Baldwin wrote informational letters about the book and sent them to a mailing list of Havanese dog owners. The demand generated by their letter writing campaign was outstanding. *The Havanese* has since won the prestigious national award, "Best Single Breed Book," and has become a surprise bestseller. Even two years after publication, this book is still selling in the top 4%.

Current top selling self-published titles include
- *Everything You Need to Know About House Training Puppies & Adult Dogs*, by Lori Verni
- *Every Rescued Dog has a Tale: Stories from the Dog Rescue Railroad,* by Deborah Eades

#15 Children

When it comes to self-published children's books, nonfiction sells much better than fiction. Unless you have an audience in which to target your promotion, children's fiction readers will have a difficult time finding your book. Consider first writing non-fiction to establish yourself as a children's author.

If you are determined to write fiction, take a tip from the author of the clever *Brandon the Bipolar Bear: A Story for Children with Bipolar Disorder.* This fiction title has been successful because it targets a real problem and appears on the Amazon screen with search terms entered by likely buyers. Parents looking for an informational book about bipolar disorder in children may end up purchasing this book when they stumble upon the title.

The books that sell best in this category teach something kids need to know or help them further understand a subject they've already been taught.

#16 Current Events

Election years see political books topping the charts, and years of economic swings find financial books dominating sales. Whatever current event you plan to report, do your research and cover your topic thoroughly. If your subject already has the public's attention people will read what you have to say. As a self-publisher you can be more responsive to trends, beating other books to the market.

A well-timed book on a hot topic can become an overnight success. Books that include time sensitive material or controversial subjects are areas where self-published titles consistently outperform their traditionally published competition. Conventional publishers can't act quickly enough to bring quick-fad books to the market, and they fear backlash from sensitive readers to books with questionable subject matter.

Current top sellers include:
- *Renewable Energy Policy,* by Paul Komor
- *Get Out Of Our House: Revolution! (A New Plan for Selecting Representatives),* Tim Cox

#17 Adult Content

Traditional publishing houses shy away from books with X-rated content. However, authors have found quite a bit of success in this genre through self-publishing. Writing about the activities of adults behind closed doors has a place in the market. You may not see your book in Barnes and Noble, but if you write something others are interested in reading, a well-written book can realize strong online sales.

8
Leveraging Amazon

Amazon.com is the single most effective sales outlet for self-published books. If you want your book to succeed in general, it must succeed on Amazon. All of the authors in chapters two and three found success not only by choosing a proven firm and writing in a successful genre, they leveraged the Amazon sales channel to sell more books. Fortunately, Amazon also provides the most cost effective book promotion tools available. This chapter will show you how to position your book to sell strongly on Amazon and how to use the tools to your greatest advantage. For more exhaustive information, check out the latest version of *Aiming at Amazon,* by Aaron Shepard.

Title Your Book to Sell

The biggest influence on how you title your book should be the impact it will have on sales. Consider your title as part of your marketing strategy. Catchy is good, but descriptive is better. The best selling self-published books are those with titles that most clearly explain the book's purpose. Great examples are:

- *A Year In the Life of an ESL (English Second Language) Student*, by Edward J. Francis
- *Teach Your Child the Multiplication Tables*, by Eugenia Francis
- *The Business Startup Checklist and Planning Guide*, by Stephanie Chandler
- *Intense Minds: Through the Eyes of Young People with Bipolar Disorder*, by Tracy Anglada
- *An Applicant's Guide to Physician Assistant School and Practice*, by Erin L. Sherer

What these titles lack in creativity, they make up for in marketing and sales. Here's why. Amazon search engines allow shoppers to type key words into a search box and immediately view a list of hundreds of likely matches. The closer your title is to the words or phrases a customer uses in a search, the more likely Amazon will be to present your book. I know authors who spend a great deal of time and research crafting titles that are most likely to match common searches. These authors know the value of sales and prefer a clumsy title that sells over a clever one that doesn't.

For example, a how-to book on becoming a police officer could easily be titled, *Joining the Force.* The title pertains to the subject and sounds adequate. The limitation with this title is that it leaves the buyer with unanswered questions. Is this a Star Wars book? Is it about what happens to new officers in the police force? Is it a novel or a personal story? Alternatively, *Becoming a Police Officer: An Insider's Guide to a Career in Law* tells the buyer exactly what to expect and it happens to be a top-seller.

Amazon experts construct the most effective titles and subtitles. When creating his title *Sell Your Book on Amazon: Top Secret Tips Guaranteed to Increase Sales for Print-On-Demand and Self-Publishing Writers*, author Brent Sampson chose each word and phrase with careful deliberation. He included the words and phrases most commonly used in Amazon searches for books about publishing. Note his title tells exactly what the book is about, and in his subtitle are phrases like "increase sales", "print-on-demand", and "self-publishing".

Aaron Shepard took his title further with *Aiming at Amazon: The NEW Business of Self Publishing, or How to Publish Books for Less, Sell Without Hassle, and Double Your Profit (or More) With Print on Demand and Book Marketing on Amazon.com.* Yes, that is the title of just one book. It's a mouthful and it isn't pretty, but it's hard to argue with results. Both of these books have been selling in the top 5% for nearly three years.

Cover Design

When designing a book cover, it's never a bad idea to look at your competition to get a feel for what is selling in a particular genre. For example, if the top selling books in your subject use three colors and black and white on their covers, you can follow their lead, just be sure to use your own fonts, layout, and colors. It's okay to be inspired, but never copy another design.

The main title should be in large bold letters that can easily be read when Amazon shrinks a picture of your book cover down to an inch for the website listing. Keep in mind, without a magnifying glass held to the computer monitor, viewers will have a difficult time reading all of the tiny words in your subtitle, especially if it's as long as this book recommends. Consider omitting the subtitle from the front cover altogether or making the font much smaller, reserving larger letters for the main title.

To ensure your book stands out against the white background of the Amazon website, consider an outline around the cover (as used for this book), or use a colored background for your cover rather than white.

Keep graphics minimal and basic. Avoid any kind of background or graphic that looks like it came from a greeting card with valleys and sunsets. Those types of covers scream inexperience. Instead, stick to clean lines and professional presentation. Two great sources for graphics (if you choose to use them) are bigstockphoto.com and istockphoto.com. They offer inexpensive royalty-free images that can be used for book covers. Just be sure the image doesn't compete with the words in your title. And remember, it's okay not to use images at all.

Book Detail Page

When a customer clicks on your title in the search results list, your book's Detail Page will pop up. On this page, customers will find most of the pertinent information about your book including the ISBN, page count, reviews your book has received, and a brief description of the book. The Book Detail Page is an opportunity for you to create a sales pitch. You are allowed up to 300 words in the book description section where you may also include other information such as a website, business name, credentials, and endorsements.

Search Words and Tags

Amazon allows anyone (including authors) to submit search terms for the products they sell. Though they often change the name of this feature, it always works in a similar way. Currently, on Amazon, the search terms feature is called *Tags*. You can find this section about half way down your book's detail page where anyone can enter likely search terms that will help customers find your book.

Amazon allows users to apply dozens of tags to a particular product, but only displays the ten or so most popular. Wisely choose nine or ten words and phrases specific to your book and add them to the search tags. Let's say you've written a guide to ski resorts. You can enter the names of specific resorts like *Aspen*, general phrases like *best ski destinations*, and generic terms such as *ski, resort,* or *vacation guide*.

Customer Reviews

You need customer reviews of your book, and the more the better. As soon as your book is available, send out free copies to friends, family, and anyone interested in your topic including other authors and thought leaders on your subject. Request a review on Amazon from those who liked your book.

You can also solicit reviews from other Amazon reviewers. One way is to approach people who have reviewed books for your competitors. Email addresses can be found in reviewer profiles, which you can click directly into from one of their reviews. You can also find the top Amazon reviewers at: **www.amazon.com/gp/customer-reviews/top-reviewers.**

Write "Request for Review" in the subject line, and keep the email brief. Let people know that you will be happy to send them a free copy once they reply with a mailing address. Never ask a reviewer to incur shipping or other costs. In my experience, 20-30% of people agree to a review.

In addition to leaving reviews, customers have the option to vote reviews as helpful or not helpful. Often, though not always, the review with the greatest number of "helpful" votes is the first review presented to shoppers. Vote the best reviews you receive as helpful, and in the event you experience a negative review you think is unfair, take it up with Amazon at **www.community-help@amazon.com.**

Reviews of Other Books

You can promote your book on Amazon by leaving reviews for other books. One of the most effective ways is to leave well-written reviews for the best-selling books in your genre. If your review is valuable to others, it will receive more helpful votes, which will increase the likelihood of shoppers reading your review over others. When you post your name at the end of the review, follow it with "author of (your book title here)".

Keep your reviews honest but positive. Nothing is less appealing to a reader than suffering through a review written by an obviously jealous competitor. If you do this, your book will be subject to revenge reviews from those same authors whose books you insulted. Keeping reviews professional will reflect well on you and your book.

Once you get the hang of it, give reviews for all of the books you've read that compete with yours. Free publicity has never been so easy.

Author Profile Page

If you decide to use a picture of yourself on the back of your book, use that same picture for your author photo on Amazon and any other promotional materials including other books you publish. When establishing yourself as an author, it's helpful to brand yourself with your audience. This is much easier if people see the same picture every time and can begin to recognize you.

Your Author Profile page on Amazon should include any books you've published in the past as well as credentials that qualify you to write the books you have published. If you don't have too much to say early in your writing career, it's okay to be brief. The profile should sound confident and strong without being boastful or self-aggrandizing.

Amazon Blog

An easy way to boost the credibility and visibility of your Book Detail Page is with a blog. A blog allows you to communicate with your readers and persuade potential customers. The three most recent blog entries are displayed for all to see right under the book description, so the quality of your writing is far more important than the number of posts.

Viewers will be able to read entries before purchasing and will quickly form ideas about the value of your book based on the content of your blog. Therefore, you should post entries only if you plan to offer your best writing with relevant content. Commonly, authors use blogs to write words of advice, tips related to their books, or announce upcoming promotional events. Blogs can serve as a forum for communication between authors and readers. If you don't want customers to post comments on your blog, you can disable that feature.

Effective blogs make the Book Detail Page more robust and professional. Well written entries bring a feeling of activity and interest to the page, which can increase the perceived popularity of a book for potential buyers. At minimum, you should consider posting at least one entry to give yourself an advantage over the sparsely filled Book Detail Pages of your competitors. Only one percent of authors take advantage of this free tool.

Listmania! And So You'd Like To…

At the time of this printing, Amazon suspended its promotion of Listmania and So You'd Like To…, but because things come and go so often at Amazon, you never know when either or both of them may return. For that reason, I've included the descriptions from the previous edition of this book:

Listmania allows Amazon users to create lists of their favorite books. For example, a professional photographer might create a list of his or her favorite books on photography techniques. A more obscure list might include someone's favorite books about chickens (the chicken list is one of the top rated lists on Amazon). Viewers can rate lists as helpful or not helpful, just like the book reviews. When searching for books on Amazon, you may notice Listmania lists recommended for your viewing. Amazon presents lists that are relevant to the book you are viewing or the search words you are using.

Clever authors promote their own books by including them in lists that they create. Because Amazon presents lists to viewers based on search words, it makes sense to create lists of books that pertain to your topic. For example, an author of a diet book might create a list titled *25 Healthy Choices You Can Make Today*. The author would include top selling diet books, as well as his or her own book, on the list. The more lists you create, the greater the chances your title will be seen.

Listmania allows viewers to click on an individual book title and go directly to its Detail Page. The more your list is selected and books within it are chosen, the more often your list will be presented. This frequency is boosted further if readers rate your list as helpful. People are more likely to click on already familiar titles, so be sure to include bestselling books in your genre.

So You'd Like to ...Guides

So You'd Like To...Guides provide another way to create a list of books on Amazon. These guides work very much like Listmania. Viewers can rate both of them as helpful or not helpful, viewers can click on the titles in both, and both target customers based on search words and previous orders. As of this writing, the top two Guides are *So You'd Like to Become a Tea Connoisseur* and *So You'd Like to Study Korean Religion*. As expected, both lists contain books that help someone go about doing those things.

The same rules for Listmania apply to the Guides. In order for Amazon to display your Guide, it must be relevant, valuable, and popular. So You'd Like to... Guides require more input from the author than Listmania because the creator leaves comments, descriptions, and opinions about each item. The extra effort weeds out most writers, leaving less competition and more room for yours to shine.

See Inside the Book

Commonly referred to as Search Inside, this service is Amazon's answer to looking before you buy. It enables a shopper to view the back cover, table of contents, index, and certain pages of a book. According to Amazon, books that use Search Inside see stronger sales.

Search Inside also makes your book available for Amazon Upgrade, which allows customers who've already purchased your book the opportunity to access an electronic version for an additional fee. Though the fee is small, you will receive a percentage of the purchase, and because the reader has already purchased your book, you have nothing to lose by participating.

Customers will be able to read their electronic copy from any internet-enabled computer. This differs from typical eBook publishing because the customer must purchase a hard copy of your book prior to viewing an electronic version. Your book will be protected because it cannot be downloaded or shared. Customers likely to use this feature are those needing information fast or who want to start reading right away.

Accuracy

An Amazon listing with misspelled words in the title, publisher, or author name will make it difficult for customers to find your book. As soon as your book is for sale on Amazon, check everything from publication dates, to ISBNs, to the spelling of every word on the page. Take quick action to correct errors. It's not always as easy as contacting Amazon about the mistakes. If the publisher or distributor has provided the inaccurate information, you'll have to contact them as well.

9
Promotion

Though marketing efforts are always necessary for generating book sales, many authors have found that by leveraging the tools available on Amazon and by sending review copies to several targeted recipients, they achieved the level of success they wanted. Nevertheless, the more promotion you give your book, the more books you will sell.

Many of the firms in this book offer marketing services for an additional fee. This chapter shows you how to execute the same promotional and marketing services offered by your publishing firm on your own and for less money. In addition to the approaches covered here, I encourage you to pursue modern day, online marketing strategies that most self-publishers have yet to implement. They are far less expensive and often more effective.

An outstanding book on internet marketing is, *Plug Your Book! Online Book Marketing for Authors,* by Steve Weber.

Blogging and Social Networking

The biggest trend in book marketing is through social networking and blogging. You can set up your own blog as well as a networking page on a site like MySpace.com and post your expert information on a daily, weekly, or monthly basis.

If that sounds like more than you're up for, consider posting on existing blogs in your genre. You can help answer questions for those in need and post your own valuable information. The key to successful blog promotion is to offer knowledge rather than a plug for your book.

You can add your book title and even a link to your Amazon sales page to your signature for each blog entry. Explore the internet for blogs that cover your topic, and make regular contributions. The best thing about blogging and networking—it's free!

Review Copies

Sometimes a press release or blog entry will lead to requests for a free copy of your book for review. One way to fulfill these requests is to purchase books at the author discount provided by your firm and send them out on your own. Alternatively, you can order the books from Amazon and have them shipped directly to the reviewer, saving yourself a trip to the post office and boosting your Amazon sales rank at the same time.

Send review copies to anyone in your industry who can help promote your book. Selecting precise targets will save your time and money. Call or email the person you wish to approach, tell them a short bit about your book, and ask if they would like to receive a review copy. Good candidates are magazines, websites, and blogs that speak to your audience. You will find the best results when you target those that cover your subject on a full-time basis.

You can also send review copies of your book before final publication to ask for blurbs from experts and supporters. Blurbs can be used on the back of the book cover and on your Amazon Book Detail Page. When targeted to appropriate recipients who are expecting a book, review copies are an inexpensive way to gain promotion.

Resist the lazy temptation to send out hundreds of unsolicited review copies. You might feel productive, but those books will land in the trash. If you send review copies, plan to do it well. Tremendous competition for attention demands your best work if you want to be noticed.

Press Releases

Because thousands of individuals and businesses compete for press attention each day, most press releases to mainstream media outlets don't generate any attention. A press release will compete with releases from every other writer, business, website, actor, musician, and model, making it nearly impossible to be noticed. Exhaust other marketing strategies before pursuing this one.

If you decide to use mainstream media press releases in your marketing strategy, commit to sending out a minimum of four releases over the course of a year and make them exceptional. It's too easy and common for authors to waste money on marketing that generates nothing.

Posters, Bookmarks, and Postcards

Unless you can explain in specific terms how these products will sell more books or increase your publicity, skip the cost of having them printed.

A Website for Your Book

A website is a great way to promote your book and launch into other businesses related to your writing. Many of the firms in this book offer a book promotion page on their sites, but most charge an exorbitant fee for a website all your own. Fortunately, online services like Web.com, GoDaddy.com, or BuildYourSite.com make it easy to set up a website yourself.

Dozens of other companies can be found with a basic Google search. They all work in a similar way. You first search availability for the domain name of your choosing. The cost on GoDaddy is $9.99 a year for the domain name. An additional $4.99 a month buys five web pages, an email account associated with the domain, as well as the features listed below.

- Choice of professionally designed templates.
- Shopping Cart Integration for sales directly from your website.
- Search engine optimization.
- Choice of 8,000 stock images.
- Website forums for interactive reader discussions.

Online marketing services and listing with major search engines are also available for much less than your publishing firm will charge.

Google Adwords

If you've ever done an internet search through Google, you're familiar with the ads that appear on the right-hand side and sometimes at the top of the results page. These ads are surprisingly inexpensive to run and can have a dramatic impact on sales. Through the Adwords website, you can set up your ad to take people to your book's website or straight to the detail page on Amazon. You pay per click and have total control over how long the ad runs and with which searches your ad will be placed. Even if you don't make Adwords a permanent fixture in your marketing efforts, it is a great way to launch a new book. To get started, go to:

www.adwords.google.com

Newswire Services

Newswire services deliver mass distribution of press releases to a wide range of mainstream media outlets. Although these services can ensure your release will be *available* to thousands of contacts, count on a well written release to get the attention of journalists. Because so many people compete for coverage, no newswire service can guarantee that the media will use your release.

Though I encourage you to research other companies, this section briefly covers services provided by PRWeb.com, Ereleases.com, and Gebbie.com. Use these as a baseline when examining other press release services, including those offered by your publisher.

PRWeb.com

PRWeb is one of the largest news distribution services with access to 100,000 journalists, industry analysts, media outlets, and newsrooms. You can pay for and post your release right on their website. The website is a little tricky and the pricing listed is not as straight forward as it first appears, so pay close attention when using this company.

Several options and packages are available starting at $80 for a very basic media blitz. Different packages allow you to choose up to ten industry specific targets. A top of the line release will cost around $780.

Options include
- Search engine optimization to increase visibility in search engines like Google and Yahoo.
- Distribution to industry specific websites and blogs.
- Guaranteed distribution through the Associated Press and top US newspapers and media outlets.
- Distribution to Bloomberg, Dow Jones, and Reuters.
- GoogleNews and YahooNews.

- Tracking analysis to show where your release has been read.

Ereleases.com

A smaller company than PRWeb, Ereleases boasts quality over quantity. Their database contacts have subscribed to receive press releases on an opt-in basis. Because they communicate with interested journalists, Ereleases claims to reach more than 95% of their sources directly at personal email addresses.

A flat fee of $399 sends your release to 30,000 opt-in journalists and editors. Also included are PR Newswire, MSN.com, AOL.com, Lycos, GoogleNews, YahooNews, and many other big online media companies. The fee also includes these added bonuses:

- Distribution to more than 17,000 newspapers, radio, and TV outlets.
- Submission to Dow Jones, Reuters, Bloomberg, The New York Times, The Wall Street Journal, Associated Press, USA Today, and Investor's Business Daily.
- Two levels of editing.
- Transmission to over 4,000 web sites, databases, and online services.
- RSS feed inclusion (through partner PR Newswire).
- WireWatch™ confirms your distribution by emailing you links to your release as it appears on several websites.

Ereleases offers great bang for the buck, delivering expansive media exposure in addition to editing services for just $399. This great deal will be hard for your publisher to beat.

Gebbie.com

A strategy of multiple press releases with focused marketing on specific outlets will be well served by Gebbie.com. For $565, you get a full year of access to more than 23,000 media listings. Media outlets include newspapers, radio, TV, consumer magazines, trade publications, news syndicates, and more. You can search the listings for publications that target a specific market, or you can go for a broader reach. Magazine listings are broken down into 115 different categories, making it easy to find publications in your genre. Each listing contains all of the contact information you need to get your message out, including:

- Mailing address
- Phone number
- Fax number
- Email address
- Website
- Circulation figures
- Network affiliation
- Metro market rank
- Readership profiles

Gebbie's software converts the contact information and your written content into a press release for email or postal mail. The service includes a mailing label wizard, mail merge, email and fax campaigns, and unlimited custom reports. See their user-friendly website for more details.

Gebbie.com is an attractive option because of the hands-on approach and control the user has choosing recipients. Access for an entire year makes it affordable to produce multiple targeted press releases.

Writing a Press Release or Posting a Blog Entry

While this may surprise you, the release of your book is not actually interesting to anyone outside your circle of friends and family. If you want attention from the media or internet community, your release or blog entry must be packaged as valuable and interesting information.

People are willing to spend time reading things they feel are interesting or that affect their lives. An announcement that you wrote a book does neither. A brief article with appeal or significance to your target audience will have far more impact than a general announcement to the world.

Instead of writing about the release of your alcoholism recovery book, weigh in as an expert on the subject. Your book may be a personal journey, but your release or post will garner more attention if the angle is the shortage of treatment options available or new strategies for successful recovery, for instance. If you have written a book about personal finance, for example, create a release about economic problems people are facing today and use your expertise to provide a solution.

Tactfully mention your book in the signature of your blog entry or in the byline of your press release. This will place you as an expert in the field while also promoting your book.

Bonus Chapter
Money and Taxes

We all want to make money on our writing, but that also means paying taxes on our earnings at the end of the year. This chapter will explain the tax issues you can expect to encounter, as well as how to get the most out of your tax deductions. Always check with your accountant if you are unsure about reporting or deducting. If you do your own taxes, I recommend using a program like TurboTax or TaxCut (around $35) to ensure you haven't overlooked something, be it a taxable event or a possible deduction. Nearly all self-publishing firms pay authors as independent contractors. This means a few things:

1. The payments you receive will be for the entire amount you have earned in royalties with no taxes withheld.
2. You will owe the IRS money based on what you earned for the year.
3. You don't have to keep track of your earnings on your own. At the end of the year, you will receive a form from your publisher to be included with your tax filings. The form will show how much money you received for the year.

4. You may offset the money you owe the IRS by deducting expenses incurred in the process of writing, researching, and marketing your book.

The IRS requires you to document all deductions with an invoice or receipt. In order to comply, you will need to start documenting your expenses right away. Don't worry—it's much easier than you think.

Easy Deductions

If you are not familiar with tax deductions, I assure you they are easy to track and easy to report. The IRS has a form (called a schedule C) where you fill in the amount of each deduction, total them up, then subtract the total dollar amount from your taxable income. Your tax payment is calculated after the deductions are subtracted, resulting in a lower payment. Depending on your income and expenses, deductions can save you hundreds to thousands of dollars in tax payments. If you are employed at a job where taxes are withheld, deductions can increase the amount of your tax return.

Keep more of your hard-earned money by taking advantage of the many tax benefits that are available to you as a writer. The list below includes the most basic and common deductions for self-published writers.

Home Office

If you do most of your writing at home, you likely have a space the IRS will consider a home office. A home office can be an entire room in your home or just a portion of a room. If the room you use is exclusively for work (not a spare bedroom), you can deduct the entire space. If you don't have a room all to yourself, you can still deduct the square footage of the space you are using. For example, if your home office is part of a spare bedroom or a corner of a room, determine the square footage of the space you use for writing.

Once you've determined the square footage of the room or part of the room used for work, divide that number by the square footage of your entire home. You will come up with a fraction, which is the percentage of your home used for work. Say you live in 2000 square foot house and your workspace is ten feet by ten feet, or one-hundred square feet. Divide 100 by 2000 and you get .05, or 5%. The percentage you arrive at is the percentage of your total home expenses that can be deducted. In this example, it is 5% of the following home costs:

- Rent or mortgage related expenses (interest, home insurance, and real estate taxes) for the year.
- Condo fees paid for the year.
- Renters or homeowners insurance paid for the year.
- Electricity and utility bills for the year.

At first glance, 5% doesn't seem like much of a deduction until you apply it to thousands of dollars in home costs. The IRS form will ask you for the total square footage of your house and the total square footage of your workspace. You then fill in your yearly home costs. For documentation purposes, you must keep copies of your electric and utility bills, insurance premiums, and year-end mortgage statements or a copy of your rental agreement that states your monthly rent payment.

To avoid an administrative nightmare, simply set aside a box where you can toss your monthly statements. At the end of the year, they will all be there waiting for you to add up and deduct. When April 15th rolls around, you will be glad you saved them.

Office Supplies

Whether you maintain a home office or not, you can still deduct office supplies. Highlighters, pens, staplers, envelopes, printer cartridges, paper, light bulbs, and anything you need to maintain your day-to-day office operations are considered office supplies. These items are all deductible as long as you save the receipts.

Office Furniture and Equipment

Need a new desk or bookshelves for your workspace? Be sure to keep the receipt so you can deduct the full cost. You don't have to buy cheap to qualify for tax deductions. The IRS allows for a maximum of $125,000 in office equipment deductions alone. Office furniture and equipment can include:

- Desks
- Tables
- Chairs
- File cabinets
- Shelves, cabinets, and storage items
- Computers
- Printers
- Copiers
- Fax machines
- Scanners
- Computer monitors
- Lamps

Furniture and equipment deductions aren't limited to the listed items. For example, the purchase of a camera for the exclusive purpose of photographing pictures for your book can be deducted. Purchased items must be used only for business purposes to qualify for IRS deductions. As always, you must have invoices or receipts for anything you deduct.

Education and Research

Whenever you attend a seminar to improve your skills, stay up to date on technology or trends that relate to your writing, or learn more about a writing related topic, you can deduct the cost as business related education. Writers have to conduct some level of research for almost every book they write. If you buy books or cds, attend speaking engagements or concerts, or subscribe to journals or magazines, you can deduct the cost if the items if they are for research or education.

Sometimes education and research involves travel. If you are writing a travel book or simply taking a class in another city, your travel expenses are deductible too.

Travel Related Expenses

When traveling away from home for business, all expenses related to overnight business travel can be deducted. They include:

- Train, bus, and airline tickets
- Cab fare
- Hotel and lodging for overnight travel
- Tips for wait staff, cabs, etc.
- Car rentals
- Phone calls made from the hotel or from payphones
- Dry-cleaning
- 50% of the cost of meals, even if the travel is not overnight

Overnight travel is defined as travel too far to conveniently return home at night. For example, a workshop or class in a nearby suburb of your city won't qualify for overnight travel deductions. On the other hand, a city two and a half hours away could be inconvenient for return, depending on your travel preferences. Travel expenses incurred for in-person interviews for your book, book signings, marketing efforts, education, and research are all deductible.

What happens when you mix business travel with leisure travel? Well, if the trip is primarily for work, the normal deductions still apply, but you cannot include non-work related expenses. For example, lodging, meals, and travel expenses incurred during the leisure portion of your trip cannot be deducted. If you decide to stay in the town of travel for a couple of extra days, expenses from the extra days are not deductible. On the other hand, deductions for a one week trip to a city where you plan to work for half a day can only include the expenses incurred specifically for the work event. Travel, lodging, and meals for the entire one-week trip are not deductible.

Auto and Transportation Expenses

You don't have to stay overnight to deduct everyday travel expenses. In fact, you don't even have to go far. Deductions can be taken for any type of work related transportation. Subway, bus, and cab fares can be deducted if you are traveling for work.

Drive your own car? The easiest way to deduct auto expense is based on the miles you drive. Whether you are driving to the store to buy supplies or taking a cab to your book signing event, the travel expenses are work related. If your work place is your home, you can start counting the miles when you pull out of your driveway. Otherwise, you will have to start counting miles once you reach your first work related destination, and stop counting when you reach the last one.

Keep a small date book in your car and record the distance you drive each day for work related activities. At the time of publishing this edition, the mileage deduction was $0.50 a mile. With the recent extreme fluctuations in gas prices, the

IRS has been changing the rate more than once a year, so check with the IRS at tax time for the rates.

Insurance Premiums

If you are an independent contractor or are self-employed and paying for your own health insurance, your premiums are deductible. The deduction does not apply if you are eligible for other forms of health care coverage through either your employer or your spouse's employer. If you qualify for this deduction, it can add up fast. Your total insurance premium deductions cannot exceed the total amount of your net profit earned. Talk to your accountant if you are unsure about a particular deduction.

Other Expenses

If you really want to take advantage of tax deductions, read *Home Business Tax Deductions: Keep What You Earn,* by Stephen Fishman and Diana Fitzpatrick. You can also talk to your accountant. Other deductible expenses commonly incurred by writers include:

- Software and computer programs
- Postage
- Long distance telephone calls
- A second phone line for work
- Subscriptions
- Memberships
- Legal and professional fees
- Half of your Social Security contributions

Whenever you are in doubt about a deduction, ask your accountant for clarification. For every deduction you take, you must be able to prove the expense occurred with an invoice or receipt. As long as you stay within IRS guidelines and deduct honest expenses, you can keep more money in your pocket and pay less to the IRS. The IRS makes frequent changes to their requirements so you should always consult a professional for the most up to date and accurate information.

INDEX